DATE D

POEMS AND PLAYS

POEMS AND PLAYS

by
Oliver Goldsmith

With an Introduction by
H. W. Garrod

Thomas Nelson and Sons Limited
London Edinburgh Paris Melbourne
Toronto and New York

Oliver Goldsmith was born on November 10, 1728, at Pallas, County Longford, Ireland, educated at Trinity College, Dublin, and other universities, and died in London on April 4, 1774.

He wrote poems, plays, a novel, and many essays and miscellaneous works, the most notable being " The Bee " (1759), "A Citizen of the World " (1762), " The Traveller " (1764), " Essays " (1765), " The Vicar of Wakefield " (1766), " The Good-natured Man " (1768), " The Deserted Village " (1770), and " She Stoops to Conquer " (1773).

CONTENTS

1180

INTRODUCTION

THE quality of Goldsmith's fame is attested by its successful resistance to two classes of mischief : the calculated impertinence of the prigs—such men, that is, as Boswell and Macaulay ; and the miscalculated kindness of the sentimentalists—chief among them Thackeray. The prigs, perhaps, do not greatly matter : here, as everywhere, their art is self-defeating. The sentimentalists are a more serious trouble, since it is no part of virtue to show hardness towards natures which have none of it nor could sustain it. Yet a humane criticism may so far, perhaps, assert itself against Thackeray, and the tribe of rhapsodists, as to recall that Goldsmith is primarily important as a *writer*. In the profession of a writer he achieved success after failing in almost every other profession known to man—medicine, law, the Church, keeping school, keeping shop, play-acting, flute-playing, begging. Of his adventures in these many callings the record is uncertain ; and he himself attached no exaggerated value to them as sources of experience giving reality to his writing. He had begged, or fluted, his way across Europe ; but it had taught him that " we see more of the world by travel, and more of human nature by remaining at home." * The crosses of his early years he took, it is likely, more in his proper character—the character, that is, of the " good-natured man " —than the popular accounts of him would have us to believe.

The reactions of this character upon political and

* *Present State of Polite Learning*, ch. xii.

literary circumstances are at least as interesting as the vicissitudes of Goldsmith's personal fortune. He was born in 1728. A new king had just reconfirmed Walpole in that long lease of political power to which Goldsmith liked to trace the decline of English letters. He died in 1774. The same year witnessed the accession of Louis XVI. to the throne of France, and the year following the beginning of the American War of Independence. These synchronisms have their significance for the study of a poet who touches greatness in two poems expressly composed to convey the truths of political economy. That the greatness of *The Traveller* and *The Deserted Village* is not given by their economics is easily said. Yet *The Traveller* at least is not properly placed if these are forgotten. It was begun just before this country became involved with France in the Seven Years' War; and it was finished in the months following Wilkes's attack on the King in No. 45 of the *North Briton*. The latter portion of it might be described as the reflections of a Good-natured Man overtaken by the first mutter of the storm of Human Freedom. The piece owes something to Addison's *Letter from Italy*. Both poets had begged their way across Europe; but that the ornate beggary of a pension from Lord Halifax had taught Addison anything, or had rendered him either acute or just in his observation, nothing in his poem indicates. He came back with what he took out: his pension, and the comfortable Whiggish conviction that Great Britain was the natural and exclusive home of Freedom and Good Government. Only so far as this conviction has truth or nature is there anything of either in his poem. Goldsmith brought home the poverty in which he started out; but the kingdoms of the world and their want of glory had persuaded him that government, good or bad, contributes little or nothing to man's happiness. Those parts of life, or of the heart, which " kings or laws " can materially affect are few. The grandeur of the human soul consists in its good-nature;

and those states are best governed of which the citizens are sufficiently good-natured to put up with what they are given.

The Traveller, especially the concluding portion, should be read side by side with a poem which consciously imitates parts of it—the *Descriptive Sketches* of Wordsworth. When the reader has made the comparison, he should make another equally instructive. He should read Goldsmith's essay *On the Distresses of a Common Soldier* (*Essays*, xxiv.), with its companion piece, *On the Distresses of the Poor* (*Citizen of the World*, cxix.) ; and these two pieces he should compare with the delineation of the same distresses furnished by Wordsworth's *Female Vagrant*. The strength of Goldsmith is his humour, of Wordsworth his want of it. Both made the mistake of supposing that the rest of the world were like themselves. The more serious mistake was that of Goldsmith ; for if there is a real distinction between good and bad, it is probably nowhere so obvious as in the case of " kings and laws." Men are serious in demanding justice, and it is silly to tell them not to mind. Souls gifted with that humorous Stoicism which makes Goldsmith, as a man and as a writer, so attractive are comparatively rare ; and humourless souls with red revolution in them at least a good deal commoner than Goldsmith believed. In one particular Goldsmith erred grievously : it did not occur to him that men who are good-natured enough to forgo their own rights can be fanatical in their assertion of the rights of others.

Accordingly in *The Traveller*, and in a less degree in *The Deserted Village*, the reader must be as easy-going as Goldsmith himself not to be sensible of a certain intellectual incompetence. Social and economic conditions were moving in the direction of a change greater than any since the break-up of the Middle Ages ; and to the self-imposed study of these altering conditions Goldsmith brought inaccurate observation and trivial com-

ment—the same faults, in fact, as made him, in the
circle of Dr. Johnson, a disputant almost contemptible.
In the exercise, on the other hand, of the arts of feeling
and memory (each of which has its proper genius) he
abounds in grace and truth : virtues which communicate
themselves even to his diction. His was not a crusad-
ing nature ; but he waged a humorous and effective
war against the dominant fear of the " low " in incident,
sentiment, and speech. " It were to be wished," he
writes,* " that we no longer found pleasure with the
inflated style that has for some years been looked upon
as fine writing, and which every young writer is now
obliged to adopt if he chooses to be read. We should
now dispense with loaded epithet and dressing up trifles
with dignity. . . Let us, instead of writing finely, try to
write naturally." That in verse Goldsmith is always
as good as his principles, that *The Traveller* and *The
Deserted Village* are everywhere free from conventional
diction, it would be rash to affirm. But they have
at least a purer and truer diction than the rest of the
poetry of their day. Of his prose style, the praise may
be set a good deal higher. Goldsmith was a born
writer, writing upon any subject well and easily. Boswell, it is true, has alleged that he consciously imitated
Johnson ; but the two styles are, in fact, essentially
opposed : and what Goldsmith says of " dressing up
trifles with dignity " hits Johnson hard. In the qualities required for the profession of a *general writer*, Johnson was not well endowed ; Goldsmith has all of them
in perfection. " Goldsmith," says Johnson himself,
with splendid justice, " was a man who, whatever he
wrote, did it better than any other man could do." He
essayed nothing, perhaps, which required the highest
powers ; but in the kind of writing which he undertook
he had an easy competence, a style in perfect adjust-
ment with temperament.

* *Present State of Polite Learning*, ch. x.

This volume contains, along with the poems of Goldsmith, his plays ; and certainly they are not a negligible part of his achievement. He has himself analyzed for us the faults of the fashionable comedy of the time. " The Comic Muse, long sick," was " a-dying." She was dying of her own " gentility," of her fussy fear of the " low," of her addiction to " sentimentals." These were, in a great degree, infections of literature as a whole ; and it is the grand merit of all Goldsmith's writings (a merit best illustrated, perhaps, by the *Vicar of Wakefield*) to be clean of all of them. To dispel them from contemporary comedy, however, was a business requiring a high quality of faith. Goldsmith speaks of himself as coming to Comedy " strongly prepossessed in favour of the poets of the last age." His most valuable prepossession was, in fact, one which he shares with all considerable dramatists. It is probable that he had picked up in his *Wanderjahre* some first-hand acquaintance with stage practice ; but his greatest asset was his masculine conviction that what the theatre wishes is in tragedy to be made to cry, and in comedy to be made to laugh. " On my conscience," he writes, " I believe we have all forgot to laugh in these days." Outside Goldsmith and Sheridan the eighteenth century can show no comedy at which a man could conceivably laugh. It was not done ; and it was not easy to persuade people that it should be done. *The Good-Natured Man* is not among the best English comedies ; but it at least gave Goldsmith the chance of developing a character which he understood thoroughly, and it furnished his public with a reasonable excuse for permitting themselves to be amused. " Uncommonly low," said the *London Chronicle* the next morning. But Goldsmith had made his public laugh ; and before they had time to relapse into gentility and " sentimentals," he gave them, in *She Stoops to Conquer*, one of the masterpieces of the English stage. The plot involves a ludicrous experience of his own youth, when he upon one occasion mistook the house of a gentleman in Ardagh for an inn. Nothing is so good for the world as that now and again some one should break in on its gentilities, command its best cheer, and rouse it to something of catholic innkeeping quality.

Let us not forget, however, that Goldsmith belongs after all not to the Inn (any more than to the City or the Club), but to the fields. There his treasure and his heart is. He had laid up his treasure in the long years of his vagabondage; and his most characteristic effects, those effects in which he illustrates most movingly our common nature, proceed from the pieties of youthful memory. His true spiritual riches are the poverty of his youth; and his best skill, to illumine tenderly for each of us the deserted village of the heart, its broken roads, and unfinished purposes.

H. W. GARROD.

THE TRAVELLER

POEMS AND PLAYS OF OLIVER GOLDSMITH

THE TRAVELLER:

OR, A PROSPECT OF SOCIETY

(1764)

To the Rev. Henry Goldsmith

Dear Sir,—I am sensible that the friendship between us can acquire no new force from the ceremonies of a Dedication ; and perhaps it demands an excuse thus to prefix your name to my attempts, which you decline giving with your own.   But as a part of this Poem was formerly written to you from Switzerland, the whole can now, with propriety, be only inscribed to you.   It will also throw a light upon many parts of it when the reader understands that it is addressed to a man who, despising fame and fortune, has retired early to happiness and obscurity, with an income of forty pounds a year.

I now perceive, my dear brother, the wisdom of your humble choice.   You have entered upon a sacred office, where the harvest is great and the labourers are but few ; while you have left the field of ambition, where the labourers are many, and the harvest not worth carrying away.   But of all kinds of ambition, what from the refinement of the times, from different systems of criticism, and from the divisions of party, that which pursues poetical fame is the wildest.

Poetry makes a principal amusement among unpolished nations; but in a country verging to the extremes of refinement, Painting and Music come in for a share. As these offer the feeble mind a less laborious entertainment, they at first rival Poetry, and at length supplant her; they engross all that favour once shown to her, and though but younger sisters, seize upon the elder's birthright.

Yet, however this art may be neglected by the powerful, it is still in great danger from the mistaken efforts of the learned to improve it. What criticisms have we not heard of late in favour of blank verse and Pindaric odes, choruses, anapests, and iambics, alliterative care and happy negligence! Every absurdity has now a champion to defend it: and as he is generally much in the wrong, so he has always much to say; for error is ever talkative.

But there is an enemy to this art still more dangerous —I mean party. Party entirely distorts the judgment and destroys the taste. When the mind is once infected with this disease, it can only find pleasure in what contributes to increase the distemper. Like the tiger, that seldom desists from pursuing man after having once preyed upon human flesh, the reader who has once gratified his appetite with calumny, makes ever after the most agreeable feast upon murdered reputation. Such readers generally admire some half-witted thing, who wants to be thought a bold man, having lost the character of a wise one. Him they dignify with the name of poet: his tawdry lampoons are called satires; his turbulence is said to be force, and his frenzy fire.

What reception a poem may find, which has neither abuse, party, nor blank verse to support it, I cannot tell, nor am I solicitous to know. My aims are right. Without espousing the cause of any party, I have attempted to moderate the rage of all. I have endeavoured to

show that there may be equal happiness in states that
are differently governed from our own; that each state
has a particular principle of happiness, and that this
principle in each may be carried to a mischievous excess. There are few can judge better than yourself
how far these positions are illustrated in this Poem.—
I am, dear sir, your most affectionate brother,

OLIVER GOLDSMITH.

REMOTE, unfriended, melancholy, slow,
Or by the lazy Scheld or wandering Po;
Or onward, where the rude Carinthian boor
Against the houseless stranger shuts the door;
Or where Campania's plain forsaken lies,
A weary waste expanding to the skies;
Where'er I roam, whatever realms to see,
My heart untravelled fondly turns to thee;
Still to my brother turns, with ceaseless pain,
And drags at each remove a lengthening chain.
  Eternal blessings crown my earliest friend,
And round his dwelling guardian saints attend:
Blest be that spot where cheerful guests retire
To pause from toil, and trim their evening fire:
Blest that abode where want and pain repair,
And every stranger finds a ready chair:
Blest be those feasts, with simple plenty crowned,
Where all the ruddy family around
Laugh at the jests or pranks that never fail,
Or sigh with pity at some mournful tale;
Or press the bashful stranger to his food,
And learn the luxury of doing good.
  But me, not destined such delights to share,
My prime of life in wandering spent and care;
Impelled, with steps unceasing, to pursue
Some fleeting good, that mocks me with the view;
That, like the circle bounding earth and skies,
Allures from far, yet, as I follow, flies;

My fortune leads to traverse realms alone,
And find no spot of all the world my own.

   E'en now, where Alpine solitudes ascend,
I sit me down a pensive hour to spend ;
And placed on high above the storm's career,
Look downward where an hundred realms appear ;
Lakes, forests, cities, plains extending wide,
The pomp of kings, the shepherd's humbler pride.

   When thus Creation's charms around combine,
Amidst the store, should thankless pride repine ?
Say, should the philosophic mind disdain
That good which makes each humbler bosom vain ?
Let school-taught pride dissemble all it can,
These little things are great to little man ;
And wiser he, whose sympathetic mind
Exults in all the good of all mankind.
Ye glittering towns, with wealth and splendour crowned ;
Ye fields, where summer spreads profusion round ;
Ye lakes, whose vessels catch the busy gale ;
Ye bending swains, that dress the flowery vale ;
For me your tributary stores combine :
Creation's heir, the world, the world is mine.

   As some lone miser, visiting his store,
Bends at his treasure, counts, recounts it o'er ;
Hoards after hoards his rising raptures fill,
Yet still he sighs, for hoards are wanting still :
Thus to my breast alternate passions rise,
Pleased with each good that Heaven to man supplies ;
Yet oft a sigh prevails, and sorrows fall,
To see the hoard of human bliss so small ;
And oft I wish amidst the scene to find
Some spot to real happiness consigned,
Where my worn soul, each wandering hope at rest,
May gather bliss to see my fellows blest.

   But where to find that happiest spot below
Who can direct, when all pretend to know ?
The shudd'ring tenant of the frigid zone
Boldly proclaims that happiest spot his own ;

Extols the treasures of his stormy seas,
And his long nights of revelry and ease :
The naked negro, panting at the line,
Boasts of his golden sands and palmy wine,
Basks in the glare, or stems the tepid wave,
And thanks his gods for all the good they gave.
Such is the patriot's boast where'er we roam ;
His first, best country ever is at home.
And yet, perhaps, if countries we compare,
And estimate the blessings which they share,
Though patriots flatter, still shall wisdom find
An equal portion dealt to all mankind ;
As different good, by art or nature given,
To different nations makes their blessing even.
  Nature, a mother kind alike to all,
Still grants her bliss at labour's earnest call :
With food as well the peasant is supplied
On Idra's cliffs as Arno's shelvy side ;
And though the rocky-crested summits frown,
These rocks by custom turn to beds of down.
From art more various are the blessings sent ;
Wealth, commerce, honour, liberty, content.
Yet these each other's power so strong contest,
That either seems destructive of the rest.
Where wealth and freedom reign, contentment fails ;
And honour sinks where commerce long prevails.
Hence every state, to one loved blessing prone,
Conforms and models life to that alone,
Each to the fav'rite happiness attends,
And spurns the plan that aims at other ends :
Till carried to excess in each domain,
This fav'rite good begets peculiar pain.
  But let us try these truths with closer eyes,
And trace them through the prospect as it lies :
Here for a while my proper cares resigned,
Here let me sit in sorrow for mankind ;
Like yon neglected shrub at random cast,
That shades the steep, and sighs at every blast.

Far to the right, where Apennine ascends,
Bright as the summer, Italy extends :
Its uplands sloping deck the mountain's side,
Woods over woods in gay theatric pride ;
While oft some temple's mould'ring tops between
With venerable grandeur mark the scene.
    Could Nature's bounty satisfy the breast,
The sons of Italy were surely blest.
Whatever fruits in different climes were found,
That proudly rise, or humbly court the ground ;
Whatever blooms in torrid tracts appear,
Whose bright succession decks the varied year ;
Whatever sweets salute the northern sky
With vernal lives, that blossom but to die ;
These, here disporting, own the kindred soil,
Nor ask luxuriance from the planter's toil ;
While sea-born gales their gelid wings expand
To winnow fragrance round the smiling land.
    But small the bliss that sense alone bestows,
And sensual bliss is all the nation knows.
In florid beauty groves and fields appear ;
Man seems the only growth that dwindles here.
Contrasted faults through all his manners reign :
Though poor, luxurious ; though submissive, vain ;
Though grave, yet trifling ; zealous, yet untrue ;
And e'en in penance planning sins anew.
All evils here contaminate the mind
That opulence departed leaves behind ;
For wealth was theirs, not far removed the date
When commerce proudly flourished through the state :
At her command the palace learnt to rise,
Again the long-fall'n column sought the skies,
The canvas glowed, beyond e'en nature warm,
The pregnant quarry teemed with human form,
Till, more unsteady than the southern gale,
Commerce on other shores displayed her sail ;
While nought remained of all that riches gave,
But towns unmanned, and lords without a slave ;

And late the nation found with fruitless skill
Its former strength was but plethoric ill.
   Yet still the loss of wealth is here supplied
By arts, the splendid wrecks of former pride ;
From these the feeble heart and long-fall'n mind
An easy compensation seem to find.
Here may be seen, in bloodless pomp arrayed,
The paste-board triumph and the cavalcade,
Processions formed for piety and love,
A mistress or a saint in every grove.
By sports like these are all their cares beguiled ;
The sports of children satisfy the child.
Each nobler aim, represt by long control,
Now sinks at last, or feebly mans the soul ;
While low delights succeeding fast behind,
In happier meanness occupy the mind :
As in those domes where Cæsars once bore sway,
Defaced by time and tott'ring in decay,
There in the ruin, heedless of the dead,
The shelter-seeking peasant builds his shed ;
And, wondering man could want the larger pile,
Exults, and owns his cottage with a smile.
   My soul, turn from them, turn we to survey
Where rougher climes a nobler race display ;
Where the bleak Swiss their stormy mansion tread,
And force a churlish soil for scanty bread.
No product here the barren hills afford,
But man and steel, the soldier and his sword :
No vernal blooms their torpid rocks array,
But winter lingering chills the lap of May :
No zephyr fondly sues the mountain's breast,
But meteors glare, and stormy glooms invest.
   Yet, still, e'en here content can spread a charm,
Redress the clime, and all its rage disarm.
Though poor the peasant's hut, his feasts though small,
He sees his little lot the lot of all ;
Sees no contiguous palace rear its head
To shame the meanness of his humble shed :

No costly lord the sumptuous banquet deal
To make him loathe his vegetable meal ;
But calm, and bred in ignorance and toil,
Each wish contracting fits him to the soil.
Cheerful at morn he wakes from short repose,
Breasts the keen air, and carols as he goes ;
With patient angle trolls the finny deep ;
Or drives his vent'rous ploughshare to the steep ;
Or seeks the den where snow-tracks mark the way,
And drags the struggling savage into day.
At night returning, every labour sped,
He sits him down the monarch of a shed ;
Smiles by his cheerful fire, and round surveys
His children's looks, that brighten at the blaze ;
While his loved partner, boastful of her hoard,
Displays her cleanly platter on the board :
And haply too some pilgrim, thither led,
With many a tale repays the nightly bed.

    Thus every good his native wilds impart,
Imprints the patriot passion on his heart ;
And e'en those ills that round his mansion rise
Enhance the bliss his scanty fund supplies.
Dear is that shed to which his soul conforms,
And dear that hill which lifts him to the storms ;
And as a child, when scaring sounds molest,
Clings close and closer to the mother's breast,
So the loud torrent and the whirlwind's roar
But bind him to his native mountains more.

    Such are the charms to barren states assigned ;
Their wants but few, their wishes all confined.
Yet let them only share the praises due :
If few their wants, their pleasures are but few ;
For every want that stimulates the breast
Becomes a source of pleasure when redrest ;
Whence from such lands each pleasing science flies
That first excites desire, and then supplies ;
Unknown to them, when sensual pleasures cloy,
To fill the languid pause with finer joy ;

Unknown those powers that raise the soul to flame,
Catch every nerve, and vibrate through the frame.
Their level life is but a smouldering fire,
Unquenched by want, unfanned by strong desire ;
Unfit for raptures, or, if raptures cheer
On some high festival of once a year,
In wild excess the vulgar breast takes fire,
Till, buried in debauch, the bliss expire.
   But not their joys alone thus coarsely flow :
Their morals, like their pleasures, are but low ;
For, as refinement stops, from sire to son
Unaltered, unimproved the manners run,
And love's and friendship's finely pointed dart
Fall blunted from each indurated heart.
Some sterner virtues o'er the mountain's breast
May sit, like falcons cowering on the nest ;
But all the gentler morals, such as play
Through life's more cultured walks, and charm the way,
These, far dispersed, on timorous pinions fly,
To sport and flutter in a kinder sky.
   To kinder skies, where gentler manners reign,
I turn ; and France displays her bright domain.
Gay, sprightly land of mirth and social ease,
Pleased with thyself, whom all the world can please,
How often have I led thy sportive choir,
With tuneless pipe, beside the murmuring Loire ?
Where shading elms along the margin grew,
And freshened from the wave the zephyr flew ;
And haply, though my harsh touch, falt'ring still,
But mocked all tune, and marred the dancer's skill,
Yet would the village praise my wondrous power,
And dance, forgetful of the noon-tide hour.
Alike all ages. Dames of ancient days
Have led their children through the mirthful maze,
And the gay grandsire, skilled in gestic lore,
Has frisked beneath the burthen of threescore.
   So blest a life these thoughtless realms display ;
Thus idly busy rolls their world away ;

Theirs are those arts that mind to mind endear,
For honour forms the social temper here.
Honour, that praise which real merit gains,
Or e'en imaginary worth obtains,
Here passes current : paid from hand to hand,
It shifts in splendid traffic round the land ;
From courts to camps, to cottages, it strays,
And all are taught an avarice of praise.
They please, are pleased ; they give to get esteem ;
Till, seeming blest, they grow to what they seem.
   But while this softer art their bliss supplies,
It gives their follies also room to rise ;
For praise too dearly loved, or warmly sought,
Enfeebles all internal strength of thought,
And the weak soul, within itself unblest,
Leans for all pleasure on another's breast.
Hence ostentation here, with tawdry art,
Pants for the vulgar praise which fools impart ;
Here vanity assumes her pert grimace,
And trims her robes of frieze with copper lace ;
Here beggar pride defrauds her daily cheer,
To boast one splendid banquet once a year ;
The mind still turns where shifting fashion draws,
Nor weighs the solid worth of self-applause.
   To men of other minds my fancy flies,
Embosomed in the deep where Holland lies.
Methinks her patient sons before me stand,
Where the broad ocean leans against the land,
And, sedulous to stop the coming tide,
Lift the tall rampire's artificial pride.
Onward methinks, and diligently slow,
The firm connected bulwark seems to grow ;
Spreads its long arms amidst the watery roar,
Scoops out an empire, and usurps the shore.
While the pent ocean, rising o'er the pile,
Sees an amphibious world beneath him smile :
The slow canal, the yellow-blossomed vale,
The willow-tufted bank, the gliding sail,—

The crowded mart, the cultivated plain,—
A new creation rescued from his reign.

    Thus, while around the wave-subjected soil
Impels the native to repeated toil,
Industrious habits in each bosom reign,
And industry begets a love of gain.
Hence all the good from opulence that springs,
With all those ills superfluous treasure brings,
Are here displayed.   Their much-loved wealth imparts
Convenience, plenty, elegance, and arts:
But view them closer, craft and fraud appear;
E'en liberty itself is bartered here.
At gold's superior charms all freedom flies;
The needy sell it, and the rich man buys;
A land of tyrants, and a den of slaves,
Here wretches seek dishonourable graves,
And calmly bent, to servitude conform,
Dull as their lakes that slumber in the storm.

    Heavens! how unlike their Belgic sires of old!
Rough, poor, content, ungovernably bold;
War in each breast, and freedom on each brow:
How much unlike the sons of Britain now!

    Fired at the sound, my genius spreads her wing,
And flies where Britain courts the western spring;
Where lawns extend that scorn Arcadian pride,
And brighter streams than famed Hydaspes glide.
There all around the gentlest breezes stray;
There gentle music melts on every spray;
Creation's mildest charms are there combined,
Extremes are only in the master's mind!
Stern o'er each bosom Reason holds her state,
With daring aims irregularly great;
Pride in their port, defiance in their eye,
I see the lords of human kind pass by;
Intent on high designs, a thoughtful band,
By forms unfashioned fresh from Nature's hand,
Fierce in their native hardiness of soul,
True to imagined right, above control,

While e'en the peasant boasts these rights to scan,
And learns to venerate himself as man.

Thine, Freedom, thine the blessings pictured here ;
Thine are those charms that dazzle and endear :
Too blest indeed, were such without alloy !
But fostered e'en by Freedom ills annoy :
That independence Britons prize too high
Keeps man from man, and breaks the social tie ;
The self-dependent lordlings stand alone,
All claims that bind and sweeten life unknown.
Here, by the bonds of nature feebly held,
Minds combat minds, repelling and repelled ;
Ferments arise, imprisoned factions roar,
Represt ambition struggles round her shore,
Till, over-wrought, the general system feels,
Its motions stop, or frenzy fire the wheels.

Nor this the worst.   As nature's ties decay,
As duty, love, and honour fail to sway,
Fictitious bonds, the bonds of wealth and law,
Still gather strength, and force unwilling awe.
Hence all obedience bows to these alone,
And talent sinks, and merit weeps unknown :
Till time may come, when, stript of all her charms,
The land of scholars and the nurse of arms,
Where noble stems transmit the patriot flame,
Where kings have toiled and poets wrote for fame,
One sink of level avarice shall lie,
And scholars, soldiers, kings, unhonoured die.

Yet think not, thus when Freedom's ills I state,
I mean to flatter kings, or court the great :
Ye powers of truth, that bid my soul aspire,
Far from my bosom drive the low desire.
And thou, fair Freedom, taught alike to feel
The rabble's rage and tyrant's angry steel ;
Thou transitory flower, alike undone
By proud contempt or favour's fostering sun ;
Still may thy blooms the changeful clime endure !
I only would repress them to secure :

For just experience tells, in every soil,
That those who think must govern those that toil;
And all that Freedom's highest aims can reach
Is but to lay proportioned loads on each.
Hence, should one order disproportioned grow,
Its double weight must ruin all below.
  O then how blind to all that truth requires,
Who think it freedom when a part aspires!
Calm is my soul, nor apt to rise in arms,
Except when fast approaching danger warms;
But when contending chiefs blockade the throne,
Contracting regal power to stretch their own,
When I behold a factious band agree
To call it freedom when themselves are free,
Each wanton judge new penal statutes draw,
Laws grind the poor, and rich men rule the law,
The wealth of climes where savage nations roam
Pillaged from slaves to purchase slaves at home,
Fear, pity, justice, indignation start,
Tear off reserve, and bare my swelling heart;
Till half a patriot, half a coward grown,
I fly from petty tyrants to the throne.
  Yes, brother, curse with me that baleful hour
When first ambition struck at regal power;
And thus polluting honour in its source,
Gave wealth to sway the mind with double force.
Have we not seen, round Britain's peopled shore,
Her useful sons exchanged for useless ore?
Seen all her triumphs but destruction haste,
Like flaring tapers brightening as they waste?
Seen opulence, her grandeur to maintain,
Lead stern depopulation in her train,
And over fields where scattered hamlets rose
In barren solitary pomp repose?
Have we not seen at pleasure's lordly call
The smiling long-frequented village fall?
Beheld the duteous son, the sire decayed,
The modest matron, and the blushing maid,

Forced from their homes, a melancholy train,
To traverse climes beyond the western main ;
Where wild Oswego spreads her swamps around,
And Niagara stuns with thundering sound ?
    Even now, perhaps, as there some pilgrim strays
Through tangled forests and through dangerous ways,
Where beasts with man divided empire claim,
And the brown Indian marks with murderous aim ;
There, while above the giddy tempest flies,
And all around distressful yells arise,
The pensive exile, bending with his woe,
To stop too fearful, and too faint to go,
Casts a long look where England's glories shine,
And bids his bosom sympathize with mine.
    Vain, very vain, my weary search to find
That bliss which only centres in the mind :
Why have I strayed from pleasure and repose,
To seek a good each government bestows ?
In every government, though terrors reign,
Though tyrant kings or tyrant laws restrain,
How small, of all that human hearts endure,
That part which laws or kings can cause or cure !
Still to ourselves in every place consigned,
Our own felicity we make or find :
With secret course, which no loud storms annoy,
Glides the smooth current of domestic joy.
The lifted axe, the agonizing wheel,
Luke's iron crown, and Damien's bed of steel,
To men remote from power but rarely known,
Leave reason, faith, and conscience all our own.

THE DESERTED VILLAGE

THE DESERTED VILLAGE

(1770)

To SIR JOSHUA REYNOLDS

DEAR SIR,—I can have no expectations, in an address of this kind, either to add to your reputation or to establish my own. You can gain nothing from my admiration, as I am ignorant of that art in which you are said to excel ; and I may lose much by the severity of your judgment, as few have a juster taste in poetry than you. Setting interest therefore aside, to which I never paid much attention, I must be indulged at present in following my affections. The only dedication I ever made was to my brother, because I loved him better than most other men. He is since dead. Permit me to inscribe this poem to you.

How far you may be pleased with the versification and mere mechanical parts of this attempt, I do not pretend to inquire ; but I know you will object (and indeed several of our best and wisest friends concur in the opinion) that the depopulation it deplores is nowhere to be seen, and the disorders it laments are only to be found in the poet's own imagination. To this I can scarcely make any other answer than that I sincerely believe what I have written ; that I have taken all possible pains, in my country excursions, for these four or five years past, to be certain of what I allege, and that all my views and inquiries have led me to believe those miseries real which I here attempt to display. But this is not the place to enter into an inquiry, whether the country be depopulating or not; the discussion would take up much room, and I should prove myself, at best, an indifferent politician, to tire the reader with a long preface, when I want his unfatigued attention to a long poem.

In regretting the depopulation of the country, I inveigh against the increase of our luxuries; and here also I expect the shout of modern politicians against me. For twenty or thirty years past it has been the fashion to consider luxury as one of the greatest national advantages, and all the wisdom of antiquity in that particular as erroneous. Still, however, I must remain a professed ancient on that head, and continue to think those luxuries prejudicial to states by which so many vices are introduced, and so many kingdoms have been undone. Indeed, so much has been poured out of late on the other side of the question that, merely for the sake of novelty and variety, one would sometimes wish to be in the right.—I am, dear sir, your sincere friend, and ardent admirer, OLIVER GOLDSMITH.

SWEET AUBURN! loveliest village of the plain;
Where health and plenty cheered the labouring swain,
Where smiling spring its earliest visit paid,
And parting summer's lingering blooms delayed:
Dear lovely bowers of innocence and ease,
Seats of my youth, when every sport could please,
How often have I loitered o'er thy green,
Where humble happiness endeared each scene!
How often have I paused on every charm,
The sheltered cot, the cultivated farm,
The never-failing brook, the busy mill,
The decent church that topped the neighbouring hill,
The hawthorn bush, with seats beneath the shade,
For talking age and whispering lovers made!

How often have I blest the coming day,
When toil remitting lent its turn to play,
And all the village train, from labour free,
Led up their sports beneath the spreading tree,
While many a pastime circled in the shade,
The young contending as the old surveyed ;
And many a gambol frolicked o'er the ground,
And sleights of art and feats of strength went round.
And still, as each repeated pleasure tired,
Succeeding sports the mirthful band inspired ;
The dancing pair that simply sought renown,
By holding out, to tire each other down ;
The swain mistrustless of his smutted face,
While secret laughter tittered round the place ;
The bashful virgin's side-long looks of love,
The matron's glance that would those looks reprove.
These were thy charms, sweet village ! sports like these,
With sweet succession, taught even toil to please :
These round thy bowers their cheerful influence shed :
These were thy charms—but all these charms are fled.
    Sweet smiling village, loveliest of the lawn,
Thy sports are fled, and all thy charms withdrawn ;
Amidst thy bowers the tyrant's hand is seen,
And desolation saddens all thy green :
One only master grasps the whole domain,
And half a tillage stints thy smiling plain.
No more thy glassy brook reflects the day,
But, choked with sedges, works its weedy way ;
Along thy glades, a solitary guest,
The hollow-sounding bittern guards its nest ;
Amidst thy desert walks the lapwing flies,
And tires their echoes with unvaried cries ;
Sunk are thy bowers in shapeless ruin all,
And the long grass o'ertops the mouldering wall ;
And, trembling, shrinking from the spoiler's hand,
Far, far away thy children leave the land.
    Ill fares the land, to hastening ills a prey,
Where wealth accumulates, and men decay :

Princes and lords may flourish, or may fade ;
A breath can make them, as a breath has made :
But a bold peasantry, their country's pride,
When once destroyed, can never be supplied.

A time there was, ere England's griefs began,
When every rood of ground maintained its man ;
For him light labour spread her wholesome store,
Just gave what life required, but gave no more :
His best companions, innocence and health ;
And his best riches, ignorance of wealth.

But times are altered ; trade's unfeeling train
Usurp the land and dispossess the swain ;
Along the lawn, where scattered hamlets rose,
Unwieldy wealth and cumbrous pomp repose,
And every want to opulence allied,
And every pang that folly pays to pride.
Those gentle hours that plenty bade to bloom,
Those calm desires that asked but little room,
Those healthful sports that graced the peaceful scene,
Lived in each look, and brightened all the green ;
These, far departing, seek a kinder shore,
And rural mirth and manners are no more.

Sweet Auburn ! parent of the blissful hour,
Thy glades forlorn confess the tyrant's power.
Here, as I take my solitary rounds
Amidst thy tangling walks and ruined grounds,
And, many a year elapsed, return to view
Where once the cottage stood, the hawthorn grew,
Remembrance wakes with all her busy train,
Swells at my breast, and turns the past to pain.

In all my wanderings round this world of care,
In all my griefs—and God has given my share—
I still had hopes, my latest hours to crown,
Amidst these humble bowers to lay me down ;
To husband out life's taper at the close,
And keep the flame from wasting by repose :
I still had hopes, for pride attends us still,
Amidst the swains to show my book-learned skill,

Around my fire an evening group to draw,
And tell of all I felt, and all I saw;
And, as a hare whom hounds and horns pursue
Pants to the place from whence at first he flew,
I still had hopes, my long vexations past,
Here to return—and die at home at last.

   O blest retirement, friend to life's decline,
Retreats from care, that never must be mine,
How happy he who crowns in shades like these
A youth of labour with an age of ease;
Who quits a world where strong temptations try,
And, since 'tis hard to combat, learns to fly!
For him no wretches, born to work and weep,
Explore the mine, or tempt the dangerous deep;
Nor surly porter stands in guilty state,
To spurn imploring famine from the gate;
But on he moves to meet his latter end,
Angels around befriending Virtue's friend;
Bends to the grave with unperceived decay,
While Resignation gently slopes the way;
And, all his prospects brightening to the last,
His heaven commences ere the world be past!

   Sweet was the sound, when oft at evening's close
Up yonder hill the village murmur rose.
There, as I passed with careless steps and slow,
The mingling notes came softened from below;
The swain responsive as the milk-maid sung,
The sober herd that lowed to meet their young,
The noisy geese that gabbled o'er the pool,
The playful children just let loose from school,
The watch-dog's voice that bayed the whispering wind,
And the loud laugh that spoke the vacant mind;—
These all in sweet confusion sought the shade,
And filled each pause the nightingale had made.
But now the sounds of population fail,
No cheerful murmurs fluctuate in the gale,
No busy steps the grass-grown footway tread,
For all the bloomy flush of life is fled.

All but yon widowed solitary thing,
That feebly bends beside the plashy spring :
She, wretched matron, forced in age, for bread,
To strip the brook with mantling cresses spread,
To pick her wintry faggot from the thorn,
To seek her nightly shed, and weep till morn ;
She only left of all the harmless train,
The sad historian of the pensive plain.

    Near yonder copse, where once the garden smiled,
And still where many a garden flower grows wild ;
There, where a few torn shrubs the place disclose,
The village preacher's modest mansion rose.
A man he was to all the country dear,
And passing rich with forty pounds a year ;
Remote from towns he ran his godly race,
Nor e'er had changed, nor wished to change, his place ;
Unpractised he to fawn, or seek for power,
By doctrines fashioned to the varying hour ;
Far other aims his heart had learned to prize,
More skilled to raise the wretched than to rise.
His house was known to all the vagrant train ;
He chid their wanderings, but relieved their pain :
The long-remembered beggar was his guest,
Whose beard descending swept his aged breast ;
The ruined spendthrift, now no longer proud,
Claimed kindred there, and had his claims allowed ;
The broken soldier, kindly bade to stay,
Sat by his fire, and talked the night away,
Wept o'er his wounds or tales of sorrow done,
Shouldered his crutch, and showed how fields were won.
Pleased with his guests, the good man learned to glow,
And quite forgot their vices in their woe ;
Careless their merits or their faults to scan,
His pity gave ere charity began.

    Thus to relieve the wretched was his pride,
And e'en his failings leaned to virtue's side ;
But in his duty prompt at every call,
He watched and wept, he prayed and felt for all ;

And, as a bird each fond endearment tries
To tempt its new-fledged offspring to the skies,
He tried each art, reproved each dull delay,
Allured to brighter worlds, and led the way.

Beside the bed where parting life was laid,
And sorrow, guilt, and pain, by turns dismayed,
The reverend champion stood. At his control
Despair and anguish fled the struggling soul;
Comfort came down the trembling wretch to raise,
And his last faltering accents whispered praise.

At church, with meek and unaffected grace,
His looks adorned the venerable place;
Truth from his lips prevailed with double sway,
And fools, who came to scoff, remained to pray.
The service past, around the pious man,
With steady zeal, each honest rustic ran;
E'en children followed with endearing wile,
And plucked his gown, to share the good man's smile.
His ready smile a parent's warmth exprest;
Their welfare pleased him, and their cares distrest:
To them his heart, his love, his griefs were given,
But all his serious thoughts had rest in heaven.
As some tall cliff that lifts its awful form,
Swells from the vale, and midway leaves the storm,
Though round its breast the rolling clouds are spread,
Eternal sunshine settles on its head.

Beside yon straggling fence that skirts the way,
With blossomed furze unprofitably gay,
There, in his noisy mansion, skilled to rule,
The village master taught his little school.
A man severe he was, and stern to view;
I knew him well, and every truant knew:
Well had the boding tremblers learned to trace
The day's disasters in his morning face;
Full well they laughed with counterfeited glee
At all his jokes, for many a joke had he;
Full well the busy whisper circling round
Conveyed the dismal tidings when he frowned.

Yet he was kind, or, if severe in aught,
The love he bore to learning was in fault ;
The village all declared how much he knew :
'Twas certain he could write, and cipher too ;
Lands he could measure, terms and tides presage,
And e'en the story ran that he could gauge :
In arguing, too, the parson owned his skill ;
For e'en though vanquished, he could argue still ;
While words of learned length and thundering sound
Amazed the gazing rustics ranged around ;
And still they gazed, and still the wonder grew,
That one small head could carry all he knew.
    But past is all his fame.   The very spot
Where many a time he triumphed is forgot.
Near yonder thorn, that lifts its head on high,
Where once the sign-post caught the passing eye,
Low lies that house where nut-brown draughts inspired,
Where grey-beard mirth and smiling toil retired,
Where village statesmen talked with looks profound,
And news much older than their ale went round.
Imagination fondly stoops to trace
The parlour splendours of that festive place :
The white-washed wall, the nicely sanded floor,
The varnished clock that clicked behind the door ;
The chest contrived a double debt to pay,
A bed by night, a chest of drawers by day ;
The pictures placed for ornament and use,
The twelve good rules, the royal game of goose ;
The hearth, except when winter chilled the day,
With aspen boughs and flowers and fennel gay ;
While broken tea-cups, wisely kept for show,
Ranged o'er the chimney, glistened in a row.
    Vain transitory splendours ! could not all
Reprieve the tottering mansion from its fall ?
Obscure it sinks, nor shall it more impart
An hour's importance to the poor man's heart.
Thither no more the peasant shall repair
To sweet oblivion of his daily care ;

No more the farmer's news, the barber's tale,
No more the woodman's ballad shall prevail ;
No more the smith his dusky brow shall clear,
Relax his ponderous strength, and lean to hear ;
The host himself no longer shall be found
Careful to see the mantling bliss go round ;
Nor the coy maid, half willing to be prest,
Shall kiss the cup to pass it to the rest.

   Yes ! let the rich deride, the proud disdain,
These simple blessings of the lowly train ;
To me more dear, congenial to my heart,
One native charm, than all the gloss of art ;
Spontaneous joys, where Nature has its play,
The soul adopts, and owns their first-born sway ;
Lightly they frolic o'er the vacant mind,
Unenvied, unmolested, unconfined.
But the long pomp, the midnight masquerade,
With all the freaks of wanton wealth arrayed,—
In these, ere triflers half their wish obtain,
The toiling pleasure sickens into pain ;
And, e'en while fashion's brightest arts decoy,
The heart distrusting asks if this be joy.

   Ye friends to truth, ye statesmen who survey
The rich man's joys increase, the poor's decay,
'Tis yours to judge, how wide the limits stand
Between a splendid and a happy land.
Proud swells the tide with loads of freighted ore,
And shouting Folly hails them from her shore ;
Hoards e'en beyond the miser's wish abound,
And rich men flock from all the world around.
Yet count our gains. This wealth is but a name
That leaves our useful products still the same.
Not so the loss. The man of wealth and pride
Takes up a space that many poor supplied ;
Space for his lake, his park's extended bounds,
Space for his horses, equipage, and hounds :
The robe that wraps his limbs in silken sloth
Has robbed the neighbouring fields of half their growth ;

His seat, where solitary sports are seen,
Indignant spurns the cottage from the green :
Around the world each needful product flies,
For all the luxuries the world supplies ;
While thus the land adorned for pleasure all
In barren splendour feebly waits the fall.

As some fair female unadorned and plain,
Secure to please while youth confirms her reign,
Slights every borrowed charm that dress supplies,
Nor shares with art the triumph of her eyes ;
But when those charms are past, for charms are frail
When time advances, and when lovers fail,
She then shines forth, solicitous to bless,
In all the glaring impotence of dress.
Thus fares the land by luxury betrayed :
In Nature's simplest charms at first arrayed,
But verging to decline, its splendours rise,
Its vistas strike, its palaces surprise ;
While, scourged by famine from the smiling land,
The mournful peasant leads his humble band,
And while he sinks, without one arm to save,
The country blooms—a garden and a grave.

Where then, ah ! where, shall poverty reside,
To 'scape the pressure of contiguous pride ?
If to some common's fenceless limits strayed
He drives his flock to pick the scanty blade,
Those fenceless fields the sons of wealth divide,
And even the bare-worn common is denied.

If to the city sped—what waits him there ?
To see profusion that he must not share ;
To see ten thousand baneful arts combined
To pamper luxury, and thin mankind ;
To see those joys the sons of pleasure know
Extorted from his fellow-creature's woe.
Here while the courtier glitters in brocade,
There the pale artist plies the sickly trade ;
Here while the proud their long-drawn pomps display,
There the black gibbet glooms beside the way.

The dome where pleasure holds her midnight reign
Here richly decked admits the gorgeous train :
Tumultuous grandeur crowds the blazing square,
The rattling chariots clash, the torches glare.
Sure scenes like these no troubles e'er annoy !
Sure these denote one universal joy !
Are these thy serious thoughts ?—Ah, turn thine eyes
Where the poor houseless shivering female lies.
She once, perhaps, in village plenty blest,
Has wept at tales of innocence distrest ;
Her modest looks the cottage might adorn,
Sweet as the primrose peeps beneath the thorn ;
Now lost to all ; her friends, her virtue fled,
Near her betrayer's door she lays her head,
And, pinched with cold, and shrinking from the shower,
With heavy heart deplores that luckless hour,
When idly first, ambitious of the town,
She left her wheel and robes of country brown.
    Do thine, sweet Auburn,—thine, the loveliest train,—
Do thy fair tribes participate her pain ?
Even now, perhaps, by cold and hunger led,
At proud men's doors they ask a little bread !
    Ah, no ! To distant climes, a dreary scene,
Where half the convex world intrudes between,
Through torrid tracts with fainting steps they go,
Where wild Altama murmurs to their woe.
Far different there from all that charmed before,
The various terrors of that horrid shore ;
Those blazing suns that dart a downward ray,
And fiercely shed intolerable day ;
Those matted woods, where birds forget to sing,
But silent bats in drowsy clusters cling ;
Those poisonous fields with rank luxuriance crowned,
Where the dark scorpion gathers death around,
Where at each step the stranger fears to wake
The rattling terrors of the vengeful snake,
Where crouching tigers wait their hapless prey,
And savage men more murderous still than they ;

While oft in whirls the mad tornado flies,
Mingling the ravaged landscape with the skies.
Far different these from every former scene,
The cooling brook, the grassy vested green,
The breezy covert of the warbling grove,
That only sheltered thefts of harmless love.

Good Heaven! what sorrows gloomed that parting day,
That called them from their native walks away;
When the poor exiles, every pleasure past,
Hung round the bowers, and fondly looked their last,
And took a long farewell, and wished in vain
For seats like these beyond the western main,
And shuddering still to face the distant deep,
Returned and wept, and still returned to weep.
The good old sire the first prepared to go
To new-found worlds, and wept for others' woe;
But for himself, in conscious virtue brave,
He only wished for worlds beyond the grave.
His lovely daughter, lovelier in her tears,
The fond companion of his helpless years,
Silent went next, neglectful of her charms,
And left a lover's for a father's arms.
With louder plaints the mother spoke her woes,
And blest the cot where every pleasure rose,
And kissed her thoughtless babes with many a tear,
And clasped them close, in sorrow doubly dear,
Whilst her fond husband strove to lend relief
In all the silent manliness of grief.

O luxury! thou curst by Heaven's decree,
How ill exchanged are things like these for thee!
How do thy potions, with insidious joy,
Diffuse their pleasures only to destroy!
Kingdoms by thee, to sickly greatness grown,
Boast of a florid vigour not their own.
At every draught more large and large they grow,
A bloated mass of rank unwieldy woe;
Till sapped their strength, and every part unsound,
Down, down they sink, and spread a ruin round.

Even now the devastation is begun,
And half the business of destruction done ;
Even now, methinks, as pondering here I stand,
I see the rural virtues leave the land.
Down where yon anchoring vessel spreads the sail,
That idly waiting flaps with every gale,
Downward they move, a melancholy band,
Pass from the shore, and darken all the strand.
Contented toil, and hospitable care,
And kind connubial tenderness, are there ;
And piety with wishes placed above,
And steady loyalty, and faithful love.
And thou, sweet Poetry, thou loveliest maid,
Still first to fly where sensual joys invade ;
Unfit in these degenerate times of shame
To catch the heart, or strike for honest fame ;
Dear charming nymph, neglected and decried,
My shame in crowds, my solitary pride ;
Thou source of all my bliss, and all my woe,
That found'st me poor at first, and keep'st me so ;
Thou guide by which the nobler arts excel,
Thou nurse of every virtue, fare thee well !
Farewell, and O ! where'er thy voice be tried,
On Torno's cliffs, or Pambamarca's side,
Whether where equinoctial fervours glow,
Or winter wraps the polar world in snow,
Still let thy voice, prevailing over time,
Redress the rigours of the inclement clime ;
Aid slighted truth with thy persuasive strain ;
Teach erring man to spurn the rage of gain :
Teach him, that states of native strength possest,
Though very poor, may still be very blest ;
That trade's proud empire hastes to swift decay,
As ocean sweeps the laboured mole away ;
While self-dependent power can time defy,
As rocks resist the billows and the sky.

THE HERMIT: A BALLAD

THE HERMIT: A BALLAD

(1766)

THE following letter, addressed to the printer of the *St. James's Chronicle*, appeared in that paper in June 1767 :—

SIR,—As there is nothing I dislike so much as newspaper controversy, particularly upon trifles, permit me to be as concise as possible in informing a correspondent of yours, that I recommended *Blainville's Travels* because I thought the book was a good one ; and I think so still. I said I was told by the bookseller that it was then first published : but in that, it seems, I was misinformed, and my reading was not extensive enough to set me right.

Another correspondent of yours accuses me of having taken a ballad I published some time ago from one by the ingenious Mr. Percy. I do not think there is any great resemblance between the two pieces in question. If there be any, his ballad is taken from mine. I read it to Mr. Percy some years ago ; and he (as we both considered these things as trifles at best) told me with his usual good humour, the next time I saw him, that he had taken my plan to form the fragments of Shakespeare into a ballad of his own. He then read me his little Cento, if I may so call it, and I highly approved it. Such petty anecdotes as these are scarce worth printing : and, were it not for the busy disposition of some of your correspondents, the public should never have known that he owes me the hint of his ballad, or that I am obliged to his friendship and learning for communications of a much more important nature.— I am, sir, yours, etc.   OLIVER GOLDSMITH.

" TURN, gentle Hermit of the dale,
    And guide my lonely way
To where yon taper cheers the vale
    With hospitable ray.

" For here forlorn and lost I tread,
    With fainting steps and slow,
Where wilds, immeasurably spread,
    Seem lengthening as I go."

" Forbear, my son," the Hermit cries,
    " To tempt the dangerous gloom ;
For yonder faithless phantom flies
    To lure thee to thy doom.

" Here to the houseless child of want
    My door is open still ;
And though my portion is but scant,
    I give it with good will.

" Then turn to-night, and freely share
    Whate'er my cell bestows,
My rushy couch and frugal fare,
    My blessing and repose.

" No flocks that range the valley free
    To slaughter I condemn ;
Taught by that Power that pities me,
    I learn to pity them :

" But from the mountain's grassy side
   A guiltless feast I bring,
A scrip with herbs and fruits supplied,
   And water from the spring.

" Then, pilgrim, turn ; thy cares forego ;
   All earth-born cares are wrong :
Man wants but little here below,
   Nor wants that little long."

Soft as the dew from heaven descends
   His gentle accents fell :
The modest stranger lowly bends,
   And follows to the cell.

Far in a wilderness obscure
   The lonely mansion lay,
A refuge to the neighbouring poor
   And strangers led astray.

No stores beneath its humble thatch
   Required a master's care ;
The wicket, opening with a latch,
   Received the harmless pair.

And now, when busy crowds retire
   To take their evening rest,
The Hermit trimmed his little fire,
   And cheered his pensive guest.

And spread his vegetable store,
   And gaily pressed, and smiled ;
And skilled in legendary lore
   The lingering hours beguiled.

Around in sympathetic mirth
   Its tricks the kitten tries ;
The cricket chirrups in the hearth ;
   The crackling faggot flies.

But nothing could a charm impart
   To soothe the stranger's woe ;
For grief was heavy at his heart,
   And tears began to flow.

His rising cares the Hermit spied,
   With answering care opprest :
" And whence, unhappy youth," he cried,
   " The sorrows of thy breast ?

" From better habitations spurned,
   Reluctant dost thou rove ?
Or grieve for friendship unreturned,
   Or unregarded love ?

" Alas ! the joys that Fortune brings
   Are trifling, and decay ;
And those who prize the trifling things
   More trifling still than they.

" And what is friendship but a name,
   A charm that lulls to sleep,
A shade that follows wealth or fame,
   But leaves the wretch to weep ?

" And love is still an emptier sound,
   The modern fair-one's jest ;
On earth unseen, or only found
   To warm the turtle's nest.

" For shame, fond youth, thy sorrows hush,
   And spurn the sex," he said :
But, while he spoke, a rising blush
   His love-lorn guest betrayed.

Surprised he sees new beauties rise,
   Swift mantling to the view ;
Like colours o'er the morning skies,
   As bright, as transient too.

The bashful look, the rising breast,
   Alternate spread alarms :
The lovely stranger stands confest
   A maid in all her charms.

" And, ah ! forgive a stranger rude,
   A wretch forlorn," she cried ;
" Whose feet unhallowed thus intrude
   Where heaven and you reside.

" But let a maid thy pity share,
   Whom love has taught to stray ;
Who seeks for rest, but finds despair
   Companion of her way.

" My father lived beside the Tyne ;
   A wealthy lord was he ;
And all his wealth was marked as mine,—
   He had but only me.

" To win me from his tender arms
   Unnumbered suitors came,
Who praised me for imputed charms,
   And felt or feigned a flame.

" Each hour a mercenary crowd
    With richest proffers strove ;
Amongst the rest young Edwin bowed,
    But never talked of love.

" In humble, simplest habits clad,
    No wealth nor power had he ;
Wisdom and worth were all he had,
    But these were all to me.

" And when beside me in the dale
    He carolled lays of love,
His breath lent fragrance to the gale,
    And music to the grove.

" The blossom opening to the day,
    The dews of heaven refined,
Could nought of purity display,
    To emulate his mind.

" The dew, the blossom on the tree.
    With charms inconstant shine ;
Their charms were his, but, woe to me !
    Their constancy was mine.

" For still I tried each fickle art,
    Importunate and vain ;
And while his passion touched my heart,
    I triumphed in his pain.

" Till quite dejected with my scorn
    He left me to my pride,
And sought a solitude forlorn,
    In secret, where he died.

" But mine the sorrow, mine the fault,
 And well my life shall pay ;
I'll seek the solitude he sought,
 And stretch me where he lay.

" And there forlorn, despairing, hid,
 I'll lay me down and die ;
'Twas so for me that Edwin did,
 And so for him will I."

" Forbid it, Heaven ! " the Hermit cried,
 And clasped her to his breast :
The wondering fair one turned to chide,—
 'Twas Edwin's self that prest.

" Turn, Angelina, ever dear ;
 My charmer, turn to see
Thy own, thy long-lost Edwin here,
 Restored to love and thee.

" Thus let me hold thee to my heart,
 And every care resign :
And shall we never, never part,
 My life—my all that's mine ?

" No, never from this hour to part,
 We'll live and love so true,
The sigh that rends thy constant heart
 Shall break thy Edwin's too."

MISCELLANEOUS POEMS

MISCELLANEOUS POEMS

THE HAUNCH OF VENISON

A POETICAL EPISTLE TO LORD CLARE

THANKS, my lord, for your venison, for finer or fatter
Never ranged in a forest, or smoked in a platter ;
The haunch was a picture for painters to study,
The fat was so white, and the lean was so ruddy ;
Though my stomach was sharp, I could scarce help
    regretting
To spoil such a delicate picture by eating ;
I had thoughts in my chambers to place it in view,
To be shown to my friends as a piece of virtù ;
As in some Irish houses, where things are so-so,
One gammon of bacon hangs up for a show :
But, for eating a rasher of what they take pride in,
They'd as soon think of eating the pan it is fried in.
But hold—let me pause—don't I hear you pronounce
This tale of the bacon a damnable bounce ?
Well, suppose it a bounce—sure a poet may try,
By a bounce now and then, to get courage to fly.
But, my lord, it's no bounce : I protest in my turn
It's a truth—and your lordship may ask Mr. Byrne.
    To go on with my tale : as I gazed on the haunch,
I thought of a friend that was trusty and staunch ;
So I cut it, and sent it to Reynolds undrest,
To paint it, or eat it, just as he liked best.
Of the neck and the breast I had next to dispose ;
'Twas a neck and a breast that might rival Monroe's :

But in parting with these I was puzzled again,
With the how, and the who, and the where, and the
    when.
There's Howard, and Coley, and H——rth, and Hiff,
I think they love venison—I know they love beef,
There's my countryman Higgins—oh ! let him alone,
For making a blunder, or picking a bone.
But hang it !—to poets who seldom can eat
Your very good mutton's a very good treat ;
Such dainties to them their health it might hurt,
It's like sending them ruffles, when wanting a shirt.
While thus I debated, in reverie centred,
An acquaintance, a friend as he called himself, entered ;
An under-bred, fine-spoken fellow was he,
And he smiled as he looked at the venison and me.
" What have we got here ?—Why this is good eating !
Your own I suppose—or is it in waiting ? "
" Why, whose should it be ? " cried I with a flounce ;
" I get these things often "—but that was a bounce :
" Some lords, my acquaintance, that settle the nation,
Are pleased to be kind—but I hate ostentation."
    " If that be the case then," cried he, very gay,
" I'm glad I have taken this house in my way.
To-morrow you take a poor dinner with me ;
No words—I insist on't—precisely at three ;
We'll have Johnson, and Burke ; all the wits will be
    there ;
My acquaintance is slight, or I'd ask my Lord Clare.
And now that I think on't, as I am a sinner !
We wanted this venison to make out the dinner.
What say you—a pasty ?   It shall, and it must,
And my wife, little Kitty, is famous for crust.
Here, porter ! this venison with me to Mile-end ;
No stirring—I beg—my dear friend—my dear friend ! "
Thus, snatching his hat, he brushed off like the wind,
And the porter and eatables followed behind.
    Left alone to reflect, having emptied my shelf,
And " nobody with me at sea but myself ; "

Though I could not help thinking my gentleman hasty,
Yet Johnson, and Burke, and a good venison pasty,
Were things that I never disliked in my life,
Though clogged with a coxcomb, and Kitty his wife.
So next day, in due splendour to make my approach,
I drove to his door in my own hackney-coach.

When come to the place where we all were to dine
(A chair-lumbered closet just twelve feet by nine),
My friend bade me welcome, but struck me quite dumb
With tidings that Johnson and Burke would not come :
" For I knew it," he cried : " both eternally fail ;
The one with his speeches, and t'other with Thrale.
But no matter, I'll warrant we'll make up the party
With two full as clever, and ten times as hearty.
The one is a Scotchman, the other a Jew ;
They're both of them merry, and authors like you ;
The one writes the 'Snarler,' the other the 'Scourge' ;
Some thinks he writes 'Cinna'—he owns to 'Panurge.'"
While thus he described them by trade and by name,
They entered, and dinner was served as they came.

At the top a fried liver and bacon were seen ;
At the bottom was tripe, in a swinging tureen ;
At the sides there was spinach and pudding made hot ;
In the middle a place where the pasty—was not.
Now, my lord, as for tripe, it's my utter aversion,
And your bacon I hate like a Turk or a Persian ;
So there I sat stuck, like a horse in a pound,
While the bacon and liver went merrily round :
But what vexed me most was that d——d Scottish rogue,
With his long-winded speeches, his smiles, and his brogue,
And, " Madam," quoth he, " may this bit be my poison,
A prettier dinner I never set eyes on ;
Pray a slice of your liver, though may I be curst,
But I've eat of your tripe till I'm ready to burst."
" The tripe ! " quoth the Jew, with his chocolate cheek ;
" I could dine on this tripe seven days in a week :
I like these here dinners so pretty and small ;
But your friend there, the doctor, eats nothing at all."

" O ! ho ! " quoth my friend, " he'll come on in a trice ;
He's keeping a corner for something that's nice :
There's a pasty."—" A pasty ! " repeated the Jew ;
" I don't care if I keep a corner for't too."
" What the de'il, mon, a pasty ! " re-echoed the Scot ;
" Though splitting, I'll still keep a corner for that."
" We'll all keep a corner," the lady cried out ;
" We'll all keep a corner," was echoed about.
While thus we resolved, and the pasty delayed,
With looks that quite petrified, entered the maid :
A visage so sad, and so pale with affright,
Waked Priam in drawing his curtains by night.
But we quickly found out—for who could mistake her ?—
That she came with some terrible news from the baker :
And so it fell out, for that negligent sloven
Had shut out the pasty on shutting his oven.
Sad Philomel thus—but let similes drop—
And now that I think on't, the story may stop.
To be plain, my good lord, it's but labour misplaced,
To send such good verses to one of your taste ;
You've got an odd something—a kind of discerning,
A relish, a taste—sickened over by learning ;
At least, it's your temper, as very well known,
That you think very slightly of all that's your own :
So, perhaps, in your habits of thinking amiss,
You may make a mistake, and think slightly of this.

DESCRIPTION OF AN AUTHOR'S BED-CHAMBER

WHERE the Red Lion, flaring o'er the way,
Invites each passing stranger that can pay,
Where Calvert's butt and Parson's black champagne
Regale the drabs and bloods of Drury Lane ;
There, in a lonely room, from bailiffs snug,
The Muse found Scroggen stretched beneath a rug.

A window, patched with paper, lent a ray,
That dimly showed the state in which he lay ;
The sanded floor that grits beneath the tread ;
The humid wall with paltry pictures spread ;
The royal Game of Goose was there in view,
And the Twelve Rules the royal martyr drew ;
The Seasons, framed with listing, found a place,
And brave Prince William showed his lamp-black face :
The morn was cold, he views with keen desire
The rusty grate unconscious of a fire :
With beer and milk arrears the frieze was scored,
And five cracked teacups dressed the chimney board :
A night-cap decked his brows instead of bay ;
A cap by night—a stocking all the day !

ELEGY ON THE DEATH OF A MAD DOG

GOOD people all, of every sort,
    Give ear unto my song ;
And if you find it wondrous short,—
    It cannot hold you long.

In Islington there was a man,
    Of whom the world might say,
That still a godly race he ran,—
    Whene'er he went to pray.

A kind and gentle heart he had,
    To comfort friends and foes ;
The naked every day he clad,—
    When he put on his clothes.

And in that town a dog was found,
    As many dogs there be,
Both mongrel, puppy, whelp, and hound,
    And curs of low degree.

This dog and man at first were friends ;
   But when a pique began,
The dog, to gain some private ends,
   Went mad, and bit the man.

Around from all the neighbouring streets
   The wondering neighbours ran,
And swore the dog had lost his wits,
   To bite so good a man.

The wound it seemed both sore and sad
   To every Christian eye ;
And while they swore the dog was mad,
   They swore the man would die.

But soon a wonder came to light,
   That showed the rogues they lied ;
The man recovered of the bite,
   The dog it was that died.

STANZAS. ON WOMAN

When lovely Woman stoops to folly,
   And finds too late that men betray,
What charm can soothe her melancholy,
   What art can wash her guilt away ?

The only art her guilt to cover,
   To hide her shame from every eye,
To give repentance to her lover,
   And wring his bosom—is, to die.

DRAMAS

SHE STOOPS TO CONQUER;

OR,

THE MISTAKES OF A NIGHT

A COMEDY

To SAMUEL JOHNSON, LL.D.

DEAR SIR,—By inscribing this slight performance to you, I do not mean so much to compliment you as myself. It may do me some honour to inform the public, that I have lived many years in intimacy with you. It may serve the interests of mankind also to inform them, that the greatest wit may be found in a character, without impairing the most unaffected piety.

I have, particularly, reason to thank you for your partiality to this performance. The undertaking a comedy not merely sentimental was very dangerous; and Mr. Colman, who saw this piece in its various stages, always thought it so. However, I ventured to trust it to the public; and, though it was necessarily delayed till late in the season, I have every reason to be grateful. —I am, dear sir, your most sincere friend and admirer,

OLIVER GOLDSMITH.

PROLOGUE

BY DAVID GARRICK, ESQ.

Enter MR. WOODWARD, *dressed in black, and holding a handkerchief to his eyes.*

EXCUSE me, sirs, I pray—I can't yet speak—
I'm crying now—and have been all the week.
" 'Tis not alone this mourning suit," good masters :
" I've that within "—for which there are no plasters !
Pray, would you know the reason why I'm crying ?
The Comic Muse, long sick, is now a-dying !
And if she goes, my tears will never stop ;
For as a player, I can't squeeze out one drop :
I am undone, that's all—shall lose my bread—
I'd rather, but that's nothing—lose my head.
When the sweet maid is laid upon the bier,
Shuter and I shall be chief mourners here.
To her a mawkish drab of spurious breed,
Who deals in sentimentals, will succeed !
Poor Ned and I are dead to all intents ;
We can as soon speak Greek as sentiments !
Both nervous grown, to keep our spirits up,
We now and then take down a hearty cup.
What shall we do ?   If Comedy forsake us,
They'll turn us out, and no one else will take us.
But why can't I be moral ?—Let me try—
My heart thus pressing—fixed my face and eye—
With a sententious look, that nothing means,
(Faces are blocks in sentimental scenes)

Thus I begin : " All is not gold that glitters,
Pleasure seems sweet, but proves a glass of bitters.
When Ignorance enters, Folly is at hand :
Learning is better far than house and land.
Let not your virtue trip ; who trips may stumble,
And virtue is not virtue, if she tumble."

I give it up—morals won't do for me ;
To make you laugh, I must play tragedy.
One hope remains—hearing the maid was ill,
A Doctor comes this night to show his skill.
To cheer her heart, and give your muscles motion,
He, in Five Draughts prepared, presents a potion :
A kind of magic charm—for be assured,
If you will swallow it, the maid is cured :
But desperate the Doctor, and her case is,
If you reject the dose, and make wry faces !
This truth he boasts, will boast it while he lives,
No poisonous drugs are mixed in what he gives.
Should he succeed, you'll give him his degree ;
If not, within he will receive no fee !
The College *you*, must his pretensions back,
Pronounce him Regular, or dub him Quack.

SHE STOOPS TO CONQUER

ACT THE FIRST

SCENE—*A Chamber in an old-fashioned House.*

Enter MRS. HARDCASTLE *and* MR. HARDCASTLE.

Mrs. Hard. I vow, Mr. Hardcastle, you're very particular. Is there a creature in the whole country but
ourselves, that does not take a trip to town now and
then, to rub off the rust a little? There's the two Miss
Hoggs, and our neighbour Mrs. Grigsby, go to take a
month's polishing every winter.

Hard. Ay, and bring back vanity and affectation to
last them the whole year. I wonder why London cannot
keep its own fools at home! In my time, the follies of

the town crept slowly among us, but now they travel faster than a stage-coach. Its fopperies come down not only as inside passengers, but in the very basket.

Mrs. Hard. Ay, your times were fine times indeed ; you have been telling us of them for many a long year. Here we live in an old rumbling mansion, that looks for all the world like an inn, but that we never see company. Our best visitors are old Mrs. Oddfish, the curate's wife, and little Cripplegate, the lame dancing-master ; and all our entertainment your old stories of Prince Eugene and the Duke of Marlborough. I hate such old-fashioned trumpery.

Hard. And I love it. I love everything that's old : old friends, old times, old manners, old books, old wine ; and I believe, Dorothy (*taking her hand*), you'll own I have been pretty fond of an old wife.

Mrs. Hard. Lord, Mr. Hardcastle, you're for ever at your Dorothys and your old wifes. You may be a Darby, but I'll be no Joan, I promise you. I'm not so old as you'd make me, by more than one good year. Add twenty to twenty, and make money of that.

Hard. Let me see ; twenty added to twenty makes just fifty and seven.

Mrs. Hard. It's false, Mr. Hardcastle ; I was but twenty when I was brought to bed of Tony, that I had by Mr. Lumpkin, my first husband ; and he's not come to years of discretion yet.

Hard. Nor ever will, I dare answer for him. Ay, you have taught him finely.

Mrs. Hard. No matter. Tony Lumpkin has a good fortune. My son is not to live by his learning. I don't think a boy wants much learning to spend fifteen hundred a year.

Hard. Learning, quotha ! a mere composition of tricks and mischief.

Mrs. Hard. Humour, my dear ; nothing but humour. Come, Mr. Hardcastle, you must allow the boy a little humour.

Hard. I'd sooner allow him a horse-pond. If burning
the footmen's shoes, frighting the maids, and worrying
the kittens be humour, he has it. It was but yester-
day he fastened my wig to the back of my chair, and
when I went to make a bow, I popped my bald head in
Mrs. Frizzle's face.

Mrs. Hard. And am I to blame ? The poor boy was
always too sickly to do any good. A school would be his
death. When he comes to be a little stronger, who knows
what a year or two's Latin may do for him ?

Hard. Latin for him ! A cat and fiddle. No, no ;
the alehouse and the stable are the only schools he'll ever
go to.

Mrs. Hard. Well, we must not snub the poor boy now,
for I believe we shan't have him long among us. Anybody that looks in his face may see he's consumptive.

Hard. Ay, if growing too fat be one of the symptoms.

Mrs. Hard. He coughs sometimes.

Hard. Yes, when his liquor goes the wrong way.

Mrs. Hard. I'm actually afraid of his lungs.

Hard. And truly so am I ; for he sometimes whoops
like a speaking trumpet—(*Tony hallooing behind the
scenes*)—O, there he goes—a very consumptive figure,
truly.

Enter TONY, *crossing the stage.*

Mrs. Hard. Tony, where are you going, my charmer ?
Won't you give papa and I a little of your company,
lovee ?

Tony. I'm in haste, mother ; I cannot stay.

Mrs. Hard. You shan't venture out this raw evening,
my dear ; you look most shockingly.

Tony. I can't stay, I tell you. The Three Pigeons
expects me down every moment. There's some fun
going forward.

Hard. Ay ; the alehouse, the old place ; I thought so.

Mrs. Hard. A low, paltry set of fellows.

Tony. Not so low, neither. There's Dick Muggins the exciseman, Jack Slang the horse doctor, little Aminadab that grinds the music-box, and Tom Twist that spins the pewter platter.

Mrs. Hard. Pray, my dear, disappoint them for one night at least.

Tony. As for disappointing them, I should not so much mind ; but I can't abide to disappoint myself.

Mrs. Hard. (*Detaining him.*) You shan't go.

Tony. I will, I tell you.

Mrs. Hard. I say you shan't.

Tony. We'll see which is strongest, you or I.

[*Exit, hauling her out.*

Hard. (*Solus.*) Ay, there goes a pair that only spoil each other. But is not the whole age in a combination to drive sense and discretion out of doors ? There's my pretty darling Kate ! the fashions of the times have almost infected her too. By living a year or two in town, she's as fond of gauze and French frippery as the best of them.

Enter MISS HARDCASTLE.

Hard. Blessings on my pretty innocence ! drest out as usual, my Kate. Goodness ! What a quantity of superfluous silk hast thou got about thee, girl ! I could never teach the fools of this age, that the indigent world could be clothed out of the trimmings of the vain.

Miss Hard. You know our agreement, sir. You allow me the morning to receive and pay visits, and to dress in my own manner ; and in the evening I put on my housewife's dress to please you.

Hard. Well, remember, I insist on the terms of our agreement ; and, by the by, I believe I shall have occasion to try your obedience this very evening.

Miss Hard. I protest, sir, I don't comprehend your meaning.

Hard. Then to be plain with you, Kate, I expect th

young gentleman I have chosen to be your husband from town this very day. I have his father's letter, in which he informs me his son is set out, and that he intends to follow himself shortly after.

Miss Hard. Indeed! I wish I had known something of this before. Bless me, how shall I behave? It's a thousand to one I shan't like him; our meeting will be so formal, and so like a thing of business, that I shall find no room for friendship or esteem.

Hard. Depend upon it, child, I'll never control your choice; but Mr. Marlow, whom I have pitched upon, is the son of my old friend, Sir Charles Marlow, of whom you have heard me talk so often. The young gentleman has been bred a scholar, and is designed for an employment in the service of his country. I am told he's a man of an excellent understanding.

Miss Hard. Is he?

Hard. Very generous.

Miss Hard. I believe I shall like him.

Hard. Young and brave.

Miss Hard. I'm sure I shall like him.

Hard. And very handsome.

Miss Hard. My dear papa, say no more (*kissing his hand*), he's mine; I'll have him.

Hard. And, to crown all, Kate, he's one of the most bashful and reserved young fellows in all the world.

Miss Hard. Eh! you have frozen me to death again. That word *reserved* has undone all the rest of his accomplishments. A reserved lover, it is said, always makes a suspicious husband.

Hard. On the contrary, modesty seldom resides in a breast that is not enriched with nobler virtues. It was the very feature in his character that first struck me.

Miss Hard. He must have more striking features to catch me, I promise you. However, if he be so young, so handsome, and so everything as you mention, I believe he'll do still. I think I'll have him.

Hard. Ay, Kate, but there is still an obstacle. It's more than an even wager he may not have you.

Miss Hard. My dear papa, why will you mortify one so ? Well, if he refuses, instead of breaking my heart at his indifference, I'll only break my glass for its flattery, set my cap to some newer fashion, and look out for some less difficult admirer.

Hard. Bravely resolved ! In the meantime I'll go prepare the servants for his reception : as we seldom see company, they want as much training as a company of recruits the first day's muster.   [*Exit.*

Miss Hard. (*Alone.*) Lud, this news of papa's puts me all in a flutter. Young, handsome : these he put last ; but I put them foremost. Sensible, good-natured ; I like all that. But then reserved and sheepish ; that's much against him. Yet can't he be cured of his timidity, by being taught to be proud of his wife ? Yes, and can't I—But I vow I'm disposing of the husband before I have secured the lover.

Enter MISS NEVILLE.

Miss Hard. I'm glad you're come, Neville, my dear. Tell me, Constance, how do I look this evening ? Is there anything whimsical about me ? Is it one of my well-looking days, child ? Am I in face to-day ?

Miss Nev. Perfectly, my dear. Yet now I look again —bless me !—sure no accident has happened among the canary birds or the gold fishes. Has your brother or the cat been meddling ? or has the last novel been too moving ?

Miss Hard. No ; nothing of all this. I have been threatened—I can scarce get it out—I have been threatened with a lover.

Miss Nev. And his name——

Miss Hard. Is Marlow.

Miss Nev. Indeed !

Miss Hard. The son of Sir Charles Marlow.

Miss Nev. As I live, the most intimate friend of Mr. Hastings, my admirer. They are never asunder. I believe you must have seen him when we lived in town.

Miss Hard. Never.

Miss Nev. He's a very singular character, I assure you. Among women of reputation and virtue he is the modestest man alive; but his acquaintance give him a very different character among creatures of another stamp: you understand me.

Miss Hard. An odd character indeed. I shall never be able to manage him. What shall I do? Pshaw, think no more of him, but trust to occurrences for success. But how goes on your own affair, my dear? has my mother been courting you for my brother Tony as usual?

Miss Nev. I have just come from one of our agreeable *tête-à-têtes*. She has been saying a hundred tender things, and setting off her pretty monster as the very pink of perfection.

Miss Hard. And her partiality is such, that she actually thinks him so. A fortune like yours is no small temptation. Besides, as she has the sole management of it, I'm not surprised to see her unwilling to let it go out of the family.

Miss Nev. A fortune like mine, which chiefly consists in jewels, is no such mighty temptation. But at any rate, if my dear Hastings be but constant, I make no doubt to be too hard for her at last. However, I let her suppose that I am in love with her son; and she never once dreams that my affections are fixed upon another.

Miss Hard. My good brother holds out stoutly. I could almost love him for hating you so.

Miss Nev. It is a good-natured creature at bottom, and I'm sure would wish to see me married to anybody but himself. But my aunt's bell rings for our afternoon's walk round the improvements. *Allons!* Courage is necessary, as our affairs are critical.

Miss Hard. " Would it were bed-time, and all were well." [*Exeunt.*

SCENE—*An Alehouse Room. Several shabby Fellows with punch and tobacco.* TONY *at the head of the table, a little higher than the rest, a mallet in his hand.*

Omnes. Hurrea! hurrea! hurrea! bravo!

First Fel. Now, gentlemen, silence for a song. The 'squire is going to knock himself down for a song.

Omnes. Ay, a song, a song!

Tony. Then I'll sing you, gentlemen, a song I made upon this alehouse, the Three Pigeons.

SONG

Let schoolmasters puzzle their brain
   With grammar, and nonsense, and learning,
Good liquor, I stoutly maintain,
   Gives *genus* a better discerning.
Let them brag of their heathenish gods,
   Their Lethes, their Styxes, and Stygians,
Their Quis, and their Quæs, and their Quods,
   They're all but a parcel of Pigeons.
          Toroddle, toroddle, toroll.

When methodist preachers come down,
   A-preaching that drinking is sinful,
I'll wager the rascals a crown,
   They always preach best with a skinful.
But when you come down with your pence,
   For a slice of their scurvy religion,
I'll leave it to all men of sense,
   But you, my good friend, are the Pigeon.
          Toroddle, toroddle, toroll.

Then come, put the jorum about,
   And let us be merry and clever,
Our hearts and our liquors are stout,
   Here's the Three Jolly Pigeons for ever.

Let some cry up woodcock or hare,
  Your bustards, your ducks, and your widgeons ;
But of all the *gay* birds in the air,
  Here's a health to the Three Jolly Pigeons.
          Toroddle, toroddle, toroll.

Omnes. Bravo, bravo !

First Fel. The 'squire has got spunk in him.

Second Fel. I loves to hear him sing, bekeays he never gives us nothing that's low.

Third Fel. O damn anything that's low, I cannot bear it.

Fourth Fel. The genteel thing is the genteel thing any time : if so be that a gentleman bees in a concatenation accordingly.

Third Fel. I likes the maxum of it, Master Muggins. What, though I am obligated to dance a bear, a man may be a gentleman for all that. May this be my poison, if my bear ever dances but to the very genteelest of tunes ; " Water Parted," or " The minuet in Ariadne."

Second Fel. What a pity it is the 'squire is not come to his own. It would be well for all the publicans within ten miles round of him.

Tony. Ecod, and so it would, Master Slang. I'd then show what it was to keep choice of company.

Second Fel. O he takes after his own father for that, To be sure old 'Squire Lumpkin was the finest gentleman I ever set my eyes on. For winding the straight horn, or beating a thicket for a hare, or a wench, he never had his fellow. It was a saying in the place, that he kept the best horses, dogs, and girls in the whole county.

Tony. Ecod, and when I'm of age, I'll be no bastard, I promise you. I have been thinking of Bet Bouncer and the miller's grey mare to begin with. But come, my boys, drink about and be merry, for you pay no reckoning. Well, Stingo, what's the matter ?

Enter Landlord.

Land. There be two gentlemen in a post-chaise at the door. They have lost their way upo' the forest; and they are talking something about Mr. Hardcastle.

Tony. As sure as can be, one of them must be the gentleman that's coming down to court my sister. Do they seem to be Londoners?

Land. I believe they may. They look woundily like Frenchmen.

Tony. Then desire them to step this way, and I'll set them right in a twinkling. (*Exit* Landlord.) Gentlemen, as they mayn't be good enough company for you, step down for a moment, and I'll be with you in the squeezing of a lemon. [*Exeunt mob.*

Tony. (*Solus.*) Father-in-law has been calling me whelp and hound this half-year. Now, if I pleased, I could be so revenged upon the old grumbletonian. But then I'm afraid—afraid of what? I shall soon be worth fifteen hundred a year, and let him frighten me out of *that* if he can.

Enter Landlord, *conducting* MARLOW *and* HASTINGS.

Mar. What a tedious uncomfortable day have we had of it! We were told it was but forty miles across the country, and we have come above threescore.

Hast. And all, Marlow, from that unaccountable reserve of yours, that would not let us inquire more frequently on the way.

Mar. I own, Hastings, I am unwilling to lay myself under an obligation to every one I meet, and often stand the chance of an unmannerly answer.

Hast. At present, however, we are not likely to receive any answer.

Tony. No offence, gentlemen. But I'm told you have been inquiring for one Mr. Hardcastle in these parts. Do you know what part of the country you are in?

Hast. Not in the least, sir, but should thank you for information.

Tony. Nor the way you came?

Hast. No, sir; but if you can inform us——

Tony. Why, gentlemen, if you know neither the road you are going, nor where you are, nor the road you came, the first thing I have to inform you is, that—you have lost your way.

Mar. We wanted no ghost to tell us that.

Tony. Pray, gentlemen, may I be so bold as to ask the place from whence you came?

Mar. That's not necessary towards directing us where we are to go.

Tony. No offence; but question for question is all fair, you know. Pray, gentlemen, is not this same Hardcastle a cross-grained, old-fashioned, whimsical fellow, with an ugly face, a daughter, and a pretty son?

Hast. We have not seen the gentleman; but he has the family you mention.

Tony. The daughter, a tall, trapesing, trolloping, talkative maypole; the son, a pretty, well-bred, agreeable youth, that everybody is fond of.

Mar. Our information differs in this. The daughter is said to be well-bred and beautiful; the son an awkward booby, reared up and spoiled at his mother's apronstring.

Tony. He-he-hem!—Then, gentlemen, all I have to tell you is, that you won't reach Mr. Hardcastle's house this night, I believe.

Hast. Unfortunate!

Tony. It's a damned long, dark, boggy, dirty, dangerous way. Stingo, tell the gentlemen the way to Mr. Hardcastle's! (*Winking upon the* Landlord.) Mr. Hardcastle's, of Quagmire Marsh, you understand me.

Land. Master Hardcastle's! Lock-a-daisy, my masters, you're come a deadly deal wrong! When you came to the bottom of the hill, you should have crossed down Squash Lane.

Mar. Cross down Squash Lane !

Land. Then you were to keep straight forward, till you came to four roads.

Mar. Come to where four roads meet ?

Tony. Ay ; but you must be sure to take only one of them.

Mar. O, sir, you're facetious.

Tony. Then keeping to the right, you are to go sideways till you come upon Crackskull Common : there you must look sharp for the track of the wheel, and go forward till you come to farmer Murrain's barn. Coming to the farmer's barn, you are to turn to the right, and then to the left, and then to the right about again, till you find out the old mill——

Mar. Zounds, man ! we could as soon find out the longitude !

Hast. What's to be done, Marlow ?

Mar. This house promises but a poor reception ; though perhaps the landlord can accommodate us.

Land. Alack, master, we have but one spare bed in the whole house.

Tony. And to my knowledge, that's taken up by three lodgers already. (*After a pause, in which the rest seem disconcerted.*) I have hit it. Don't you think, Stingo, our landlady could accommodate the gentlemen by the fire-side, with—three chairs and a bolster ?

Hast. I hate sleeping by the fire-side.

Mar. And I detest your three chairs and a bolster.

Tony. You do, do you ? then, let me see—what if you go on a mile farther, to the Buck's Head ; the old Buck's Head on the hill, one of the best inns in the whole county ?

Hast. O ho ! so we have escaped an adventure for this night, however.

Land. (*Apart to* TONY.) Sure, you ben't sending them to your father's as an inn, be you ?

Tony. Mum, you fool you. Let *them* find that out. (*To them.*) You have only to keep on straight forward,

till you come to a large old house by the roadside.
You'll see a pair of large horns over the door. That's
the sign. Drive up the yard, and call stoutly about
you.

Hast. Sir, we are obliged to you. The servants can't
miss the way ?

Tony. No, no : but I tell you, though, the landlord
is rich, and going to leave off business ; so he wants to
be thought a gentleman, saving your presence, he ! he !
he ! He'll be for giving you his company ; and, ecod,
if you mind him, he'll persuade you that his mother was
an alderman, and his aunt a justice of peace.

Land. A troublesome old blade, to be sure ; but a
keeps as good wines and beds as any in the whole country.

Mar. Well, if he supplies us with these, we shall want
no further connection. We are to turn to the right, did
you say ?

Tony. No, no ; straight forward. I'll just step myself, and show you a piece of the way. (*To the* Landlord.) Mum !

Land. Ah, bless your heart, for a sweet, pleasant——
damn'd mischievous son of a whore. [*Exeunt.*

ACT THE SECOND

SCENE—*An old-fashioned House.*

Enter HARDCASTLE, *followed by three or four awkward*
Servants.

Hard. Well, I hope you are perfect in the table
exercise I have been teaching you these three days.
You all know your posts and your places, and can show
that you have been used to good company, without ever
stirring from home.

Omnes. Ay, ay.

Hard. When company comes you are not to pop out
and stare, and then run in again, like frighted rabbits in
a warren.

Omnes. No, no.

Hard. You, Diggory, whom I have taken from the
barn, are to make a show at the side-table ; and you,
Roger, whom I have advanced from the plough, are to
place yourself behind my chair.   But you're not to stand
so, with your hands in your pockets.   Take your hands
from your pockets, Roger ; and from your head, you
blockhead you.   See how Diggory carries his hands.
They're a little too stiff, indeed, but that's no great
matter.

Dig. Ay, mind how I hold them.   I learned to hold
my hands this way when I was upon drill for the militia.
And so being upon drill——

Hard. You must not be so talkative, Diggory.   You
must be all attention to the guests.   You must hear us

talk, and not think of talking ; you must see us drink, and not think of drinking ; you must see us eat, and not think of eating.

Dig. By the laws, your worship, that's parfectly unpossible. Whenever Diggory sees yeating going forward, ecod, he's always wishing for a mouthful himself.

Hard. Blockhead ! Is not a belly-full in the kitchen as good as a belly-full in the parlour ? Stay your stomach with that reflection.

Dig. Ecod, I thank your worship, I'll make a shift to stay my stomach with a slice of cold beef in the pantry.

Hard. Diggory, you are too talkative.—Then, if I happen to say a good thing, or tell a good story at table, you must not all burst out a-laughing, as if you made part of the company.

Dig. Then ecod your worship must not tell the story of Ould Grouse in the gun-room : I can't help laughing at that—he ! he ! he !—for the soul of me. We have laughed at that these twenty years—ha ! ha ! ha !

Hard. Ha ! ha ! ha ! The story is a good one. Well, honest Diggory, you may laugh at that—but still remember to be attentive. Suppose one of the company should call for a glass of wine, how will you behave ? A glass of wine, sir, if you please (*to* DIGGORY).—Eh, why don't you move ?

Dig. Ecod, your worship, I never have courage till I see the eatables and drinkables brought upo' the table, and then I'm as bauld as a lion.

Hard. What, will nobody move ?

First Serv. I'm not to leave this pleace.

Second Serv. I'm sure it's no pleace of mine.

Third Serv. Nor mine, for sartain.

Dig. Wauns, and I'm sure it canna be mine.

Hard. You numskulls ! and so while, like your betters, you are quarrelling for places, the guests must be starved. O you dunces ! I find I must begin all over again——— But don't I hear a coach drive into the yard ? To your posts, you blockheads. I'll go in the meantime and give my old friend's son a hearty reception at the gate.

[*Exit* HARDCASTLE.

Dig. By the elevens, my pleace is gone quite out of my head.

Rog. I know that my pleace is to be everywhere.

First Serv. Where the devil is mine?

Second Serv. My pleace is to be nowhere at all; and so I'ze go about my business.

[*Exeunt* Servants, *running about as if frighted, different ways.*

Enter Servant *with candles, showing in* MARLOW *and* HASTINGS.

Serv. Welcome, gentlemen, very welcome! This way.

Hast. After the disappointments of the day, welcome once more, Charles, to the comforts of a clean room and a good fire. Upon my word, a very well-looking house; antique but creditable.

Mar. The usual fate of a large mansion. Having first ruined the master by good housekeeping, it at last comes to levy contributions as an inn.

Hast. As you say, we passengers are to be taxed to pay all these fineries. I have often seen a good side-board, or a marble chimney-piece, though not actually put in the bill, inflame a reckoning confoundedly.

Mar. Travellers, George, must pay in all places: the only difference is, that in good inns you pay dearly for luxuries; in bad inns you are fleeced and starved.

Hast. You have lived very much among them. In truth, I have been often surprised, that you who have seen so much of the world, with your natural good sense, and your many opportunities, could never yet acquire a requisite share of assurance.

Mar. The Englishman's malady. But tell me, George, where could I have learned that assurance you talk of? My life has been chiefly spent in a college or an inn, in seclusion from that lovely part of the creation that chiefly teach men confidence. I don't know that I was ever familiarly acquainted with a single modest woman—except my mother—But among females of another class, you know——

Hast. Ay, among them you are impudent enough of all conscience.

Mar. They are of *us*, you know.

Hast. But in the company of women of reputation I never saw such an idiot, such a trembler ; you look for all the world as if you wanted an opportunity of stealing out of the room.

Mar. Why, man, that's because I do want to steal out of the room. Faith, I have often formed a resolution to break the ice, and rattle away at any rate. But I don't know how, a single glance from a pair of fine eyes has totally overset my resolution. An impudent fellow may counterfeit modesty ; but I'll be hanged if a modest man can ever counterfeit impudence.

Hast. If you could but say half the fine things to them that I have heard you lavish upon the bar-maid of an inn, or even a college bed-maker——

Mar. Why, George, I can't say fine things to them ; they freeze, they petrify me. They may talk of a comet, or a burning mountain, or some such bagatelle ; but, to me, a modest woman, drest out in all her finery, is the most tremendous object of the whole creation.

Hast. Ha ! ha ! ha ! At this rate, man, how can you ever expect to marry ?

Mar. Never ; unless, as among kings and princes, my bride were to be courted by proxy. If, indeed, like an Eastern bridegroom, one were to be introduced to a wife he never saw before, it might be endured. But to go through all the terrors of a formal courtship, together with the episode of aunts, grandmothers, and cousins, and at last to blurt out the broad staring question of, Madam, will you marry me ? No, no, that's a strain much above me, I assure you.

Hast. I pity you. But how do you intend behaving to the lady you are come down to visit at the request of your father ?

Mar. As I behave to all other ladies. Bow very low, answer yes or no to all her demands—But for the rest, I don't think I shall venture to look in her face till I see my father's again.

Hast. I'm surprised that one who is so warm a friend can be so cool a lover.

Mar. To be explicit, my dear Hastings, my chief inducement down was to be instrumental in forwarding your happiness, not my own. Miss Neville loves you, the family don't know you ; as my friend you are sure of a reception, and let honour do the rest.

Hast. My dear Marlow ! But I'll suppress the emotion. Were I a wretch, meanly seeking to carry off a fortune, you should be the last man in the world I would apply to for assistance. But Miss Neville's person is all I ask, and that is mine, both from her deceased father's consent, and her own inclination.

Mar. Happy man ! You have talents and art to captivate any woman. I'm doomed to adore the sex, and yet to converse with the only part of it I despise. This stammer in my address, and this awkward prepossessing visage of mine, can never permit me to soar above the reach of a milliner's 'prentice, or one of the duchesses of Drury Lane. Pshaw ! this fellow here to interrupt us.

Enter HARDCASTLE.

Hard. Gentlemen, once more you are heartily welcome. Which is Mr. Marlow ? Sir, you are heartily welcome. It's not my way, you see, to receive my friends with my back to the fire. I like to give them a hearty reception in the old style at my gate. I like to see their horses and trunks taken care of.

Mar. (*Aside.*) He has got our names from the servants already. (*To him.*) We approve your caution

and hospitality, sir. (*To Hastings.*) I have been thinking, George, of changing our travelling dresses in the
morning. I am grown confoundedly ashamed of mine.

Hard. I beg, Mr. Marlow, you'll use no ceremony in
this house.

Hast. I fancy, Charles, you're right : the first blow is
half the battle. I intend opening the campaign with
the white and gold.

Hard. Mr. Marlow—Mr. Hastings—gentlemen—pray
be under no constraint in this house. This is Liberty
Hall, gentlemen. You may do just as you please
here.

Mar. Yet, George, if we open the campaign too fiercely
at first, we may want ammunition before it is over. I
think to reserve the embroidery to secure a retreat.

Hard. Your talking of a retreat, Mr. Marlow, puts
me in mind of the Duke of Marlborough, when we went
to besiege Denain. He first summoned the garrison——

Mar. Don't you think the *ventre d'or* waistcoat will do
with the plain brown ?

Hard. He first summoned the garrison, which might
consist of about five thousand men——

Hast. I think not : brown and yellow mix but very
poorly.

Hard. I say, gentlemen, as I was telling you, he summoned the garrison, which might consist of about five
thousand men——

Mar. The girls like finery.

Hard. Which might consist of about five thousand
men, well appointed with stores, ammunition, and other
implements of war. Now, says the Duke of Marlborough to George Brooks, that stood next to him—
you must have heard of George Brooks—I'll pawn my
dukedom, says he, but I take that garrison without
spilling a drop of blood. So——

Mar. What, my good friend, if you gave us a glass
of punch in the meantime ; it would help us to carry on
the siege with vigour.

Hard. Punch, sir ! (*Aside.*) This is the most unaccountable kind of modesty I ever met with.

Mar. Yes, sir, punch. A glass of warm punch, after our journey, will be comfortable. This is Liberty Hall, you know.

Hard. Here's a cup, sir.

Mar. (*Aside.*) So this fellow, in his Liberty Hall, will only let us have just what he pleases.

Hard. (*Taking the cup.*) I hope you'll find it to your mind. I have prepared it with my own hands, and I believe you'll own the ingredients are tolerable. Will you be so good as to pledge me, sir ? Here, Mr. Marlow, here is to our better acquaintance. (*Drinks.*)

Mar. (*Aside.*) A very impudent fellow this ! but he's a character, and I'll humour him a little. Sir, my service to you. (*Drinks.*)

Hast. (*Aside.*) I see this fellow wants to give us his company, and forgets that he's an innkeeper, before he has learned to be a gentleman.

Mar. From the excellence of your cup, my old friend, I suppose you have a good deal of business in this part of the country. Warm work, now and then, at elections, I suppose.

Hard. No, sir, I have long given that work over. Since our betters have hit upon the expedient of electing each other, there is no business " for us that sell ale."

Hast. So, then, you have no turn for politics, I find.

Hard. Not in the least. There was a time, indeed, I fretted myself about the mistakes of government, like other people ; but finding myself every day grow more angry, and the government growing no better, I left it to mend itself. Since that, I no more trouble my head about Hyder Ally, or Ally Cawn, than about Ally Croker. Sir, my service to you.

Hast. So that with eating above stairs, and drinking below, with receiving your friends within, and amusing them without, you lead a good pleasant bustling life of it.

Hard. I do stir about a great deal, that's certain. Half the differences of the parish are adjusted in this very parlour.

Mar. (*After drinking.*) And you have an argument in your cup, old gentleman, better than any in Westminster Hall.

Hard. Ay, young gentleman, that, and a little philosophy.

Mar. (*Aside.*) Well, this is the first time I ever heard of an innkeeper's philosophy.

Hast. So then, like an experienced general, you attack them on every quarter. If you find their reason manageable, you attack it with your philosophy ; if you find they have no reason, you attack them with this. Here's your health, my philosopher. (*Drinks.*)

Hard. Good, very good, thank you ; ha ! ha ! ha ! Your generalship puts me in mind of Prince Eugene, when he fought the Turks at the battle of Belgrade. You shall hear.

Mar. Instead of the battle of Belgrade, I believe it's almost time to talk about supper. What has your philosophy got in the house for supper ?

Hard. For supper, sir ! (*Aside.*) Was ever such a request to a man in his own house ?

Mar. Yes, sir, supper, sir ; I begin to feel an appetite. I shall make devilish work to-night in the larder, I promise you.

Hard. (*Aside.*) Such a brazen dog sure never my eyes beheld. (*To him.*) Why, really, sir, as for supper, I can't well tell. My Dorothy and the cook-maid settle these things between them. I leave these kind of things entirely to them.

Mar. You do, do you ?

Hard. Entirely. By the bye, I believe they are in actual consultation upon what's for supper this moment in the kitchen.

Mar. Then I beg they'll admit me as one of their privy council. It's a way I have got. When I travel, I always choose to regulate my own supper. Let the cook be called. No offence I hope, sir.

Hard. O no, sir, none in the least; yet I don't know how; our Bridget, the cook-maid, is not very communicative upon these occasions. Should we send for her, she might scold us all out of the house.

Hast. Let's see your list of the larder then. I ask it as a favour. I always match my appetite to my bill of fare.

Mar. (*To* HARDCASTLE, *who looks at them with surprise.*) Sir, he's very right, and it's my way too.

Hard. Sir, you have a right to command here. Here, Roger, bring us the bill of fare for to-night's supper: I believe it's drawn out—Your manner, Mr. Hastings, puts me in mind of my uncle, Colonel Wallop. It was a saying of his, that no man was sure of his supper till he had eaten it.

Hast. (*Aside.*) All upon the high ropes! His uncle a colonel! we shall soon hear of his mother being a justice of the peace. But let's hear the bill of fare.

Mar. (*Perusing.*) What's here? For the first course; for the second course; for the dessert. The devil, sir, do you think we have brought down a whole Joiners' Company, or the corporation of Bedford, to eat up such a supper? Two or three little things, clean and comfortable, will do.

Hast. But let's hear it.

Mar. (*Reading.*) For the first course, at the top, a pig and prune sauce.

Hast. Damn your pig, I say.

Mar. And damn your prune sauce, say I.

Hard. And yet, gentlemen, to men that are hungry, pig with prune sauce is very good eating.

Mar. At the bottom, a calf's tongue and brains.

Hast. Let your brains be knocked out, my good sir, I don't like them.

Mar. Or you may clap them on a plate by themselves. I do.

Hard. (*Aside.*) Their impudence confounds me. (*To them.*) Gentlemen, you are my guests, make what alterations you please. Is there anything else you wish to retrench or alter, gentlemen?

Mar. Item, a pork pie, a boiled rabbit and sausages, a Florentine, a shaking pudding, and a dish of tiff—taff—taffety cream.

Hast. Confound your made dishes; I shall be as much at a loss in this house as at a green and yellow dinner at the French ambassador's table. I'm for plain eating.

Hard. I'm sorry, gentlemen, that I have nothing you like, but if there be anything you have a particular fancy to——

Mar. Why, really, sir, your bill of fare is so exquisite, that any one part of it is full as good as another. Send us what you please. So much for supper. And now to see that our beds are aired, and properly taken care of.

Hard. I entreat you'll leave all that to me. You shall not stir a step.

Mar. Leave that to you! I protest, sir, you must excuse me, I always look to these things myself.

Hard. I must insist, sir, you'll make yourself easy on that head.

Mar. You see I'm resolved on it. (*Aside.*) A very troublesome fellow this, as I ever met with.

Hard. Well, sir, I'm resolved at least to attend you. (*Aside.*) This may be modern modesty, but I never saw anything look so like old-fashioned impudence.

[*Exeunt* MARLOW *and* HARDCASTLE.

Hast. (*Alone.*) So I find this fellow's civilities begin to grow troublesome. But who can be angry at those assiduities which are meant to please him? Ha! what do I see? Miss Neville, by all that's happy!

Enter MISS NEVILLE.

Miss Nev. My dear Hastings! To what unexpected good fortune, to what accident, am I to ascribe this happy meeting?

Hast. Rather let me ask the same question, as I could never have hoped to meet my dearest Constance at an inn.

Miss Nev. An inn ! sure you mistake : my aunt, my guardian, lives here. What could induce you to think this house an inn ?

Hast. My friend, Mr. Marlow, with whom I came down, and I, have been sent here as to an inn, I assure you. A young fellow, whom we accidentally met at a house hard by, directed us hither.

Miss Nev. Certainly it must be one of my hopeful cousin's tricks, of whom you have heard me talk so often ; ha ! ha ! ha !

Hast. He whom your aunt intends for you ? he of whom I have such just apprehensions ?

Miss Nev. You have nothing to fear from him, I assure you. You'd adore him, if you knew how heartily he despises me. My aunt knows it too, and has undertaken to court me for him, and actually begins to think she has made a conquest.

Hast. Thou dear dissembler ! You must know, my Constance, I have just seized this happy opportunity of my friend's visit here to get admittance into the family. The horses that carried us down are now fatigued with their journey, but they'll soon be refreshed ; and then, if my dearest girl will trust in her faithful Hastings, we shall soon be landed in France, where even among slaves the laws of marriage are respected.

Miss Nev. I have often told you, that though ready to obey you, I yet should leave my little fortune behind with reluctance. The greatest part of it was left me by my uncle, the India director, and chiefly consists in jewels. I have been for some time persuading my aunt to let me wear them. I fancy I'm very near succeeding. The instant they are put into my possession, you shall find me ready to make them and myself yours.

Hast. Perish the baubles ! Your person is all I desire. In the meantime, my friend Marlow must not be let into his mistake. I know the strange reserve of his temper is such, that if abruptly informed of it, he would instantly quit the house before our plan was ripe for execution.

Miss Nev. But how shall we keep him in the deception? Miss Hardcastle is just returned from walking; what if we still continue to deceive him?—This, this way—— [*They confer.*

Enter MARLOW.

Mar. The assiduities of these good people tease me beyond bearing. My host seems to think it ill manners to leave me alone, and so he claps not only himself, but his old-fashioned wife, on my back. They talk of coming to sup with us too; and then, I suppose, we are to run the gauntlet through all the rest of the family.—What have we got here?

Hast. My dear Charles! Let me congratulate you!—The most fortunate accident!—Who do you think is just alighted?

Mar. Cannot guess.

Hast. Our mistresses, boy, Miss Hardcastle and Miss Neville. Give me leave to introduce Miss Constance Neville to your acquaintance. Happening to dine in the neighbourhood, they called on their return to take fresh horses here. Miss Hardcastle has just stepped into the next room, and will be back in an instant. Wasn't it lucky? eh!

Mar. (*Aside.*) I have been mortified enough of all conscience, and here comes something to complete my embarrassment.

Hast. Well, but wasn't it the most fortunate thing in the world?

Mar. Oh! yes. Very fortunate—a most joyful encounter—But our dresses, George, you know are in disorder—What if we should postpone the happiness till to-morrow?—To-morrow at her own house—It will be every bit as convenient—and rather more respectful —To-morrow let it be. [*Offering to go.*

Miss Nev. By no means, sir. Your ceremony will displease her. The disorder of your dress will show the ardour of your impatience. Besides, she knows you are in the house, and will permit you to see her.

Mar. O! the devil! how shall I support it? Hem! hem! Hastings, you must not go. You are to assist me, you know. I shall be confoundedly ridiculous. Yet, hang it! I'll take courage. Hem!

Hast. Pshaw, man! it's but the first plunge, and all's over. She's but a woman, you know.

Mar. And, of all women, she that I dread most to encounter.

Enter MISS HARDCASTLE, *as returned from walking, a bonnet, etc.*

Hast. (*Introducing them.*) Miss Hardcastle, Mr. Marlow. I'm proud of bringing two persons of such merit together, that only want to know, to esteem each other.

Miss Hard. (*Aside.*) Now for meeting my modest gentleman with a demure face, and quite in his own manner. (*After a pause, in which he appears very uneasy and disconcerted.*) I'm glad of your safe arrival, sir. I'm told you had some accidents by the way.

Mar. Only a few, madam. Yes, we had some. Yes, madam, a good many accidents, but should be sorry—madam—or rather glad of any accidents—that are so agreeably concluded. Hem!

Hast. (*To him.*) You never spoke better in your whole life. Keep it up, and I'll insure you the victory.

Miss Hard. I'm afraid you flatter, sir. You that have seen so much of the finest company, can find little entertainment in an obscure corner of the country.

Mar. (*Gathering courage.*) I have lived, indeed, in the world, madam; but I have kept very little company. I have been but an observer upon life, madam, while others were enjoying it.

Miss Nev. But that, I am told, is the way to enjoy it at last.

Hast. (*To him.*) Cicero never spoke better. Once more, and you are confirmed in assurance for ever.

Mar. (*To him.*) Hem! Stand by me, then, and when I'm down, throw in a word or two, to set me up again.

Miss Hard. An observer, like you, upon life were, I fear, disagreeably employed, since you must have had much more to censure than to approve.

Mar. Pardon me, madam. I was always willing to be amused. The folly of most people is rather an object of mirth than uneasiness.

Hast. (*To him.*) Bravo, bravo. Never spoke so well in your whole life. Well, Miss Hardcastle, I see that you and Mr. Marlow are going to be very good company. I believe our being here will but embarrass the interview.

Mar. Not in the least, Mr. Hastings. We like your company of all things. (*To him.*) Zounds! George, sure you won't go? how can you leave us?

Hast. Our presence will but spoil conversation, so we'll retire to the next room. (*To him.*) You don't consider, man, that we are to manage a little *tête-à-tête* of our own. [*Exeunt.*

Miss Hard. (*After a pause.*) But you have not been wholly an observer, I presume, sir: the ladies, I should hope, have employed some part of your addresses.

Mar. (*Relapsing into timidity.*) Pardon me, madam, I—I—I—as yet have studied—only—to—deserve them.

Miss Hard. And that, some say, is the very worst way to obtain them.

Mar. Perhaps so, madam. But I love to converse only with the more grave and sensible part of the sex. But I'm afraid I grow tiresome.

Miss Hard. Not at all, sir; there is nothing I like so much as grave conversation myself; I could hear it for ever. Indeed, I have often been surprised how a man of sentiment could ever admire those light airy pleasures, where nothing reaches the heart.

Mar. It's——a disease——of the mind, madam. In

the variety of tastes there must be some who, wanting a relish——for——um—a—um.

Miss Hard. I understand you, sir. There must be some who, wanting a relish for refined pleasures, pretend to despise what they are incapable of tasting.

Mar. My meaning, madam, but infinitely better expressed. And I can't help observing——a——

Miss Hard. (*Aside.*) Who could ever suppose this fellow impudent upon some occasions? (*To him.*) You were going to observe, sir——

Mar. I was observing, madam—I protest, madam, I forget what I was going to observe.

Miss Hard. (*Aside.*) I vow and so do I. (*To him.*) You were observing, sir, that in this age of hypocrisy—something about hypocrisy, sir.

Mar. Yes, madam. In this age of hypocrisy there are few who upon strict inquiry do not—a—a—a——

Miss Hard. I understand you perfectly, sir.

Mar. (*Aside.*) Egad! and that's more than I do myself.

Miss Hard. You mean that in this hypocritical age there are few that do not condemn in public what they practise in private, and think they pay every debt to virtue when they praise it.

Mar. True, madam; those who have most virtue in their mouths, have least of it in their bosoms. But I'm sure I tire you, madam.

Miss Hard. Not in the least, sir; there's something so agreeable and spirited in your manner, such life and force—pray, sir, go on.

Mar. Yes, madam. I was saying——that there are some occasions, when a total want of courage, madam, destroys all the——and puts us——upon a—a—a——

Miss Hard. I agree with you entirely; a want of courage upon some occasions assumes the appearance of ignorance, and betrays us when we most want to excel. I beg you'll proceed.

Mar. Yes, madam. Morally speaking, madam—But

I see Miss Neville expecting us in the next room. I would not intrude for the world.

Miss Hard. I protest, sir, I never was more agreeably entertained in all my life. Pray go on.

Mar. Yes, madam, I was——But she beckons us to join her. Madam, shall I do myself the honour to attend you?

Miss Hard. Well, then, I'll follow.

Mar. (Aside.) This pretty smooth dialogue has done for me.   [*Exit.*

Miss Hard. (Alone.) Ha! ha! ha! Was there ever such a sober, sentimental interview? I'm certain he scarce looked in my face the whole time. Yet the fellow, but for his unaccountable bashfulness, is pretty well too. He has good sense, but then so buried in his fears, that it fatigues one more than ignorance. If I could teach him a little confidence, it would be doing somebody that I know of a piece of service. But who is that somebody? —That, faith, is a question I can scarce answer. [*Exit.*

Enter TONY *and* MISS NEVILLE, *followed by*
MRS. HARDCASTLE *and* HASTINGS.

Tony. What do you follow me for, cousin Con? I wonder you're not ashamed to be so very engaging.

Miss Nev. I hope, cousin, one may speak to one's own relations, and not be to blame.

Tony. Ay, but I know what sort of a relation you want to make me, though; but it won't do. I tell you, cousin Con, it won't do; so I beg you'll keep your distance, I want no nearer relationship.

[*She follows, coquetting him to the back scene.*

Mrs. Hard. Well! I vow, Mr. Hastings, you are very entertaining. There's nothing in the world I love to talk of so much as London, and the fashions, though I was never there myself.

Hast. Never there! You amaze me! From your air and manner, I concluded you had been bred all your life either at Ranelagh, St. James's, or Tower Wharf.

Mrs. Hard. O! sir, you're only pleased to say so. We country persons can have no manner at all. I'm in love with the town, and that serves to raise me above some of our neighbouring rustics; but who can have a manner, that has never seen the Pantheon, the Grotto Gardens, the Borough, and such places where the nobility chiefly resort? All I can do is to enjoy London at second-hand. I take care to know every *tête-à-tête* from the Scandalous Magazine, and have all the fashions, as they come out, in a letter from the two Miss Rickets of Crooked Lane. Pray how do you like this head, Mr. Hastings?

Hast. Extremely elegant and *dégagée*, upon my word, madam. Your friseur is a Frenchman, I suppose?

Mrs. Hard. I protest, I dressed it myself from a print in the Ladies' Memorandum Book for the last year.

Hast. Indeed! Such a head in a side-box at the play-house would draw as many gazers as my Lady Mayoress at a City Ball.

Mrs. Hard. I vow, since inoculation began, there is no such thing to be seen as a plain woman; so one must dress a little particular, or one may escape in the crowd.

Hast. But that can never be your case, madam, in any dress. (*Bowing.*)

Mrs. Hard. Yet, what signifies my dressing when I have such a piece of antiquity by my side as Mr. Hardcastle: all I can say will never argue down a single button from his clothes. I have often wanted him to throw off his great flaxen wig, and where he was bald, to plaster it over, like my Lord Pately, with powder.

Hast. You are right, madam; for, as among the ladies there are none ugly, so among the men there are none old.

Mrs. Hard. But what do you think his answer was? Why, with his usual Gothic vivacity, he said I only wanted him to throw off his wig, to convert it into a *tête* for my own wearing.

Hast. Intolerable! At your age you may wear what you please, and it must become you.

Mrs. Hard. Pray, Mr. Hastings, what do you take to be the most fashionable age about town?

Hast. Some time ago, forty was all the mode; but I'm told the ladies intend to bring up fifty for the ensuing winter.

Mrs. Hard. Seriously. Then I shall be too young for the fashion.

Hast. No lady begins now to put on jewels till she's past forty. For instance, Miss there, in a polite circle, would be considered as a child, as a mere maker of samplers.

Mrs. Hard. And yet Mrs. Niece thinks herself as much a woman, and is as fond of jewels, as the oldest of us all.

Hast. Your niece, is she? And that young gentleman, a brother of yours, I should presume?

Mrs. Hard. My son, sir. They are contracted to each other. Observe their little sports. They fall in and out ten times a day, as if they were man and wife already. (*To them.*) Well, Tony, child, what soft things are you saying to your cousin Constance this evening?

Tony. I have been saying no soft things; but that it's very hard to be followed about so. Ecod! I've not a place in the house now that's left to myself, but the stable.

Mrs. Hard. Never mind him, Con, my dear. He's in another story behind your back.

Miss Nev. There's something generous in my cousin's manner. He falls out before faces to be forgiven in private.

Tony. That's a damned confounded—crack.

Mrs. Hard. Ah! he's a sly one. Don't you think they are like each other about the mouth, Mr. Hastings? The Blenkinsop mouth to a T. They're of a size too. Back to back, my pretties, that Mr. Hastings may see you. Come, Tony.

Tony. You had as good not make me, I tell you. (*Measuring.*)

Miss Nev. O lud! he has almost cracked my head.

Mrs. Hard. O, the monster! For shame, Tony. You a man, and behave so!

Tony. If I'm a man, let me have my fortin. Ecod! I'll not be made a fool of no longer.

Mrs. Hard. Is this, ungrateful boy, all that I'm to get for the pains I have taken in your education? I that have rocked you in your cradle, and fed that pretty mouth with a spoon! Did not I work that waistcoat to make you genteel? Did not I prescribe for you every day, and weep while the receipt was operating?

Tony. Ecod! you had reason to weep, for you have been dosing me ever since I was born. I have gone through every receipt in the Complete Huswife ten times over; and you have thoughts of coursing me through Quincy next spring. But, ecod! I tell you, I'll not be made a fool of no longer.

Mrs. Hard. Wasn't it all for your good, viper? Wasn't it all for your good?

Tony. I wish you'd let me and my good alone, then. Snubbing this way when I'm in spirits. If I'm to have any good, let it come of itself; not to keep dinging it, dinging it into one so.

Mrs. Hard. That's false; I never see you when you're in spirits. No, Tony, you then go to the alehouse or kennel. I'm never to be delighted with your agreeable wild notes, unfeeling monster!

Tony. Ecod! mamma, your own notes are the wildest of the two.

Mrs. Hard. Was ever the like? But I see he wants to break my heart, I see he does.

Hast. Dear madam, permit me to lecture the young gentleman a little. I'm certain I can persuade him to his duty.

Mrs. Hard. Well, I must retire. Come, Constance, my love. You see, Mr. Hastings, the wretchedness of my situation: was ever poor woman so plagued with a dear, sweet, pretty, provoking, undutiful boy?

[*Exeunt* MRS. HARDCASTLE *and* MISS NEVILLE.

Tony. (Singing.) " There was a young man riding by, and fain would have his will.   Rang do didlo dee."——
Don't mind her.   Let her cry.   It's the comfort of her heart.   I have seen her and sister cry over a book for an hour together ;   and they said they liked the book the better the more it made them cry.

Hast. Then you're no friend to the ladies, I find, my pretty young gentleman ?

Tony. That's as I find 'um.

Hast. Not to her of your mother's choosing, I dare answer ?   And yet she appears to me a pretty well-tempered girl.

Tony. That's because you don't know her as well as I. Ecod !   I know every inch about her ; and there's not a more bitter cantankerous toad in all Christendom.

Hast. (Aside.) Pretty encouragement this for a lover !

Tony. I have seen her since the height of that.   She has as many tricks as a hare in a thicket, or a colt the first day's breaking.

Hast. To me she appears sensible and silent.

Tony. Ay, before company.   But when she's with her playmate, she's as loud as a hog in a gate.

Hast. But there is a meek modesty about her that charms me.

Tony. Yes, but curb her never so little, she kicks up, and you're flung in a ditch.

Hast. Well, but you must allow her a little beauty.— Yes, you must allow her some beauty.

Tony. Bandbox !   She's all a made-up thing, mun. Ah ! could you but see Bet Bouncer of these parts, you might then talk of beauty.   Ecod, she has two eyes as black as sloes, and cheeks as broad and red as a pulpit cushion.   She'd made two of she.

Hast. Well, what say you to a friend that would take this bitter bargain off your hands ?

Tony. Anon.

Hast. Would you thank him that would take Miss Neville, and leave you to happiness and your dear Betsy ?

Tony. Ay ; but where is there such a friend, for who would take *her* ?

Hast. I am he. If you but assist me, I'll engage to whip her off to France, and you shall never hear more of her.

Tony. Assist you! Ecod I will, to the last drop of my blood. I'll clap a pair of horses to your chaise that shall trundle you off in a twinkling, and maybe get you a part of her fortin beside, in jewels, that you little dream of.

Hast. My dear 'squire, this looks like a lad of spirit.

Tony. Come along, then, and you shall see more of my spirit before you have done with me. (*Singing.*)

> " We are the boys
> That fear no noise
> Where the thundering cannons roar."

[*Exeunt.*

ACT THE THIRD

Enter HARDCASTLE, *alone.*

Hard. What could my old friend Sir Charles mean by recommending his son as the modestest young man in town ? To me he appears the most impudent piece of brass that ever spoke with a tongue. He has taken possession of the easy-chair by the fire-side already. He took off his boots in the parlour, and desired me to see them taken care of. I'm desirous to know how his impudence affects my daughter. She will certainly be shocked at it.

Enter MISS HARDCASTLE, *plainly dressed.*

Hard. Well, my Kate, I see you have changed your dress, as I bade you ; and yet, I believe, there was no great occasion.

Miss Hard. I find such a pleasure, sir, in obeying your commands, that I take care to observe them without ever debating their propriety.

Hard. And yet, Kate, I sometimes give you some cause, particularly when I recommended my modest gentleman to you as a lover to-day.

Miss Hard. You taught me to expect something extraordinary, and I find the original exceeds the description.

Hard. I was never so surprised in my life ! He has quite confounded all my faculties !

Miss Hard. I never saw anything like it : and a man of the world too !

Hard. Ay, he learned it all abroad—what a fool was

I, to think a young man could learn modesty by travel-ling. He might as soon learn wit at a masquerade.

Miss Hard. It seems all natural to him.

Hard. A good deal assisted by bad company and a French dancing-master.

Miss Hard. Sure you mistake, papa! A French dancing-master could never have taught him that timid look—that awkward address—that bashful manner——

Hard. Whose look? whose manner, child?

Miss Hard. Mr. Marlow's: his *mauvaise honte*, his timidity, struck me at the first sight.

Hard. Then your first sight deceived you; for I think him one of the most brazen first sights that ever aston-ished my senses.

Miss Hard. Sure, sir, you rally! I never saw any one so modest.

Hard. And can you be serious? I never saw such a bouncing, swaggering puppy since I was born. Bully Dawson was but a fool to him.

Miss Hard. Surprising! He met me with a respectful bow, a stammering voice, and a look fixed on the ground.

Hard. He met me with a loud voice, a lordly air, and a familiarity that made my blood freeze again.

Miss Hard. He treated me with diffidence and respect; censured the manners of the age; admired the prudence of girls that never laughed; tired me with apologies for being tiresome; then left the room with a bow, and " Madam, I would not for the world detain you."

Hard. He spoke to me as if he knew me all his life before; asked twenty questions, and never waited for an answer; interrupted my best remarks with some silly pun; and when I was in my best story of the Duke of Marlborough and Prince Eugene, he asked if I had not a good hand at making punch. Yes, Kate, he asked your father if he was a maker of punch!

Miss Hard. One of us must certainly be mistaken.

Hard. If he be what he has shown himself, I'm deter-mined he shall never have my consent.

Miss Hard. And if he be the sullen thing I take him, he shall never have mine.

Hard. In one thing then we are agreed—to reject him.

Miss Hard. Yes: but upon conditions. For if you should find him less impudent, and I more presuming— if you find him more respectful, and I more importunate —I don't know—the fellow is well enough for a man— Certainly, we don't meet many such at a horse-race in the country.

Hard. If we should find him so——But that's impossible. The first appearance has done my business. I'm seldom deceived in that.

Miss Hard. And yet there may be many good qualities under that first appearance.

Hard. Ay, when a girl finds a fellow's outside to her taste, she then sets about guessing the rest of his furniture. With her, a smooth face stands for good sense, and a genteel figure for every virtue.

Miss Hard. I hope, sir, a conversation begun with a compliment to my good sense, won't end with a sneer at my understanding?

Hard. Pardon me, Kate. But if young Mr. Brazen can find the art of reconciling contradictions, he may please us both, perhaps.

Miss Hard. And as one of us must be mistaken, what if we go to make further discoveries?

Hard. Agreed. But depend on't I'm in the right.

Miss Hard. And depend on't I'm not much in the wrong. [*Exeunt.*

Enter TONY, *running in with a casket.*

Tony. Ecod! I have got them. Here they are. My cousin Con's necklaces, bobs and all. My mother shan't cheat the poor souls out of their fortin neither. O! my genus, is that you?

Enter HASTINGS.

Hast. My dear friend, how have you managed with

your mother ? I hope you have amused her with pretending love for your cousin, and that you are willing to be reconciled at last ? Our horses will be refreshed in a short time, and we shall soon be ready to set off.

Tony. And here's something to bear your charges by the way (*giving the casket*) ; your sweetheart's jewels. Keep them : and hang those, I say, that would rob you of one of them.

Hast. But how have you procured them from your mother ?

Tony. Ask me no questions, and I'll tell you no fibs. I procured them by the rule of thumb. If I had not a key to every drawer in mother's bureau, how could I go to the alehouse so often as I do ? An honest man may rob himself of his own at any time.

Hast. Thousands do it every day. But to be plain with you ; Miss Neville is endeavouring to procure them from her aunt this very instant. If she succeeds, it will be the most delicate way at least of obtaining them.

Tony. Well, keep them, till you know how it will be. But I know how it will be well enough ; she'd as soon part with the only sound tooth in her head.

Hast. But I dread the effects of her resentment, when she finds she has lost them.

Tony. Never you mind her resentment, leave *me* to manage that. I don't value her resentment the bounce of a cracker. Zounds ! here they are. Morrice ! Prance !
[*Exit* HASTINGS.

Enter MRS. HARDCASTLE *and* MISS NEVILLE.

Mrs. Hard. Indeed, Constance, you amaze me. Such a girl as you want jewels ! It will be time enough for jewels, my dear, twenty years hence, when your beauty begins to want repairs.

Miss Nev. But what will repair beauty at forty, will certainly improve it at twenty, madam.

Mrs. Hard. Yours, my dear, can admit of none. That natural blush is beyond a thousand ornaments. Besides, child, jewels are quite out at present. Don't you see half the ladies of our acquaintance, my Lady Kill-day-light, and Mrs. Crump, and the rest of them, carry their jewels to town, and bring nothing but paste and mar-casites back.

Miss Nev. But who knows, madam, but somebody that shall be nameless would like me best with all my little finery about me ?

Mrs. Hard. Consult your glass, my dear, and then see if, with such a pair of eyes, you want any better sparklers. What do you think, Tony, my dear ? does your cousin Con want any jewels in your eyes to set off her beauty ?

Tony. That's as thereafter may be.

Miss Nev. My dear aunt, if you knew how it would oblige me.

Mrs. Hard. A parcel of old-fashioned rose and table-cut things. They would make you look like the court of King Solomon at a puppet-show. Besides, I believe, I can't readily come at them. They may be missing, for aught I know to the contrary.

Tony. (*Apart to* Mrs. HARDCASTLE.) Then why don't you tell her so at once, as she's so longing for them ? Tell her they're lost. It's the only way to quiet her. Say they're lost, and call me to bear witness.

Mrs. Hard. (*Apart to* TONY.) You know, my dear, I'm only keeping them for you. So if I say they're gone, you'll bear me witness, will you ? He ! he ! he !

Tony. Never fear me. Ecod ! I'll say I saw them taken out with my own eyes.

Miss Nev. I desire them but for a day, madam. Just to be permitted to show them as relics, and then they may be locked up again.

Mrs. Hard. To be plain with you, my dear Constance, if I could find them you should have them. They're missing, I assure you. Lost, for aught I know ; but we must have patience wherever they are.

Miss Nev. I'll not believe it ! this is but a shallow

pretence to deny me. I know they are too valuable to be so slightly kept, and as you are to answer for the loss——

Mrs. Hard. Don't be alarmed, Constance. If they be lost, I must restore an equivalent. But my son knows they are missing, and not to be found.

Tony. That I can bear witness to. They are missing, and not to be found; I'll take my oath on't.

Mrs. Hard. You must learn resignation, my dear; for though we lose our fortune, yet we should not lose our patience. See me, how calm I am.

Miss Nev. Ay, people are generally calm at the misfortunes of others.

Mrs. Hard. Now I wonder a girl of your good sense should waste a thought upon such trumpery. We shall soon find them; and in the meantime you shall make use of my garnets till your jewels be found.

Miss Nev. I detest garnets.

Mrs. Hard. The most becoming things in the world to set off a clear complexion. You have often seen how well they look upon me. You *shall* have them. [*Exit.*

Miss Nev. I dislike them of all things. You shan't stir.—Was ever anything so provoking, to mislay my own jewels, and force me to wear her trumpery?

Tony. Don't be a fool. If she gives you the garnets, take what you can get. The jewels are your own already. I have stolen them out of her bureau, and she does not know it. Fly to your spark, he'll tell you more of the matter. Leave me to manage her.

Miss Nev. My dear cousin!

Tony. Vanish. She's here, and has missed them already. [*Exit* Miss Neville.] Zounds! how she fidgets and spits about like a Catherine wheel.

Enter Mrs. Hardcastle.

Mrs. Hard. Confusion! thieves! robbers! we are cheated, plundered, broke open, undone.

Tony. What's the matter, what's the matter, mamma ? I hope nothing has happened to any of the good family !

Mrs. Hard. We are robbed. My bureau has been broken open, the jewels taken out, and I'm undone.

Tony. Oh ! is that all ? Ha ! ha ! ha ! By the laws, I never saw it acted better in my life. Ecod, I thought you was ruined in earnest, ha ! ha ! ha !

Mrs. Hard. Why, boy, I *am* ruined in earnest. My bureau has been broken open, and all taken away.

Tony. Stick to that : ha ! ha ! ha ! stick to that. I'll bear witness, you know ; call me to bear witness.

Mrs. Hard. I tell you, Tony, by all that's precious, the jewels are gone, and I shall be ruined for ever.

Tony. Sure I know they are gone, and I'm to say so.

Mrs. Hard. My dearest Tony, but hear me. They're gone, I say.

Tony. By the laws, mamma, you make me for to laugh, ha ! ha ! I know who took them well enough, ha ! ha ! ha !

Mrs. Hard. Was there ever such a blockhead, that can't tell the difference between jest and earnest ? I tell you I'm not in jest, booby.

Tony. That's right, that's right ; you must be in a bitter passion, and then nobody will suspect either of us. I'll bear witness that they are gone.

Mrs. Hard. Was there ever such a cross-grained brute, that won't hear me ? Can you bear witness that you're no better than a fool ? Was ever poor woman so beset with fools on one hand, and thieves on the other ?

Tony. I can bear witness to that.

Mrs. Hard. Bear witness again, you blockhead you, and I'll turn you out of the room directly. My poor niece, what will become of her ? Do you laugh, you unfeeling brute, as if you enjoyed my distress ?

Tony. I can bear witness to that.

Mrs. Hard. Do you insult me, monster ? I'll teach you to vex your mother, I will.

Tony. I can bear witness to that.

[*He runs off, she follows him.*

Enter MISS HARDCASTLE *and* Maid.

Miss Hard. What an unaccountable creature is that brother of mine, to send them to the house as an inn ! ha ! ha ! I don't wonder at his impudence.

Maid. But what is more, madam, the young gentleman, as you passed by in your present dress, asked me if you were the bar-maid. He mistook you for the bar-maid, madam.

Miss Hard. Did he ? Then as I live, I'm resolved to keep up the delusion. Tell me, Pimple, how do you like my present dress ? Don't you think I look something like Cherry in the Beaux Stratagem ?

Maid. It's the dress, madam, that every lady wears in the country, but when she visits or receives company.

Miss Hard. And are you sure he does not remember my face or person ?

Maid. Certain of it.

Miss Hard. I vow, I thought so ; for, though we spoke for some time together, yet his fears were such, that he never once looked up during the interview. Indeed, if he had, my bonnet would have kept him from seeing me.

Maid. But what do you hope from keeping him in his mistake ?

Miss Hard. In the first place, I shall be seen, and that is no small advantage to a girl who brings her face to market. Then I shall perhaps make an acquaintance, and that's no small victory gained over one who never addresses any but the wildest of her sex. But my chief aim is, to take my gentleman off his guard, and, like an invisible champion of romance, examine the giant's force before I offer to combat.

Maid. But are you sure you can act your part, and disguise your voice so that he may mistake that, as he has already mistaken your person ?

Miss Hard. Never fear me. I think I have got the true bar cant—Did your honour call ?—Attend the Lion there—Pipes and tobacco for the Angel.—The Lamb has been outrageous this half-hour.

Maid. It will do, madam. But he's here. [*Exit* Maid.

Enter MARLOW.

Mar. What a bawling in every part of the house ! I have scarce a moment's repose. If I go to the best room, there I find my host and his story : if I fly to the gallery, there we have my hostess with her curtsey down to the ground. I have at last got a moment to myself, and now for recollection. [*Walks and muses.*

Miss Hard. Did you call, sir ? Did your honour call ?

Mar. (*Musing.*) As for Miss Hardcastle, she's too grave and sentimental for me.

Miss Hard. Did your honour call ? (*She still places herself before him, he turning away.*)

Mar. No, child. (*Musing.*) Besides, from the glimpse I had of her, I think she squints.

Miss Hard. I'm sure, sir, I heard the bell ring.

Mar. No, no. (*Musing.*) I have pleased my father, however, by coming down, and I'll to-morrow please myself by returning.

[*Taking out his tablets, and perusing.*

Miss Hard. Perhaps the other gentleman called, sir ?

Mar. I tell you, no.

Miss Hard. I should be glad to know, sir. We have such a parcel of servants !

Mar. No, no, I tell you. (*Looks full in her face.*) Yes, child, I think I did call. I wanted—I wanted—I vow, child, you are vastly handsome.

Miss Hard. O la, sir, you'll make one ashamed.

Mar. Never saw a more sprightly malicious eye. Yes.

yes, my dear, I did call. Have you got any of your—a —what d'ye call it in the house ?

Miss Hard. No, sir, we have been out of that these ten days.

Mar. One may call in this house, I find, to very little purpose. Suppose I should call for a taste, just by way of a trial, of the nectar of your lips ; perhaps I might be disappointed in that too.

Miss Hard. Nectar ! nectar ! That's a liquor there's no call for in these parts. French, I suppose. We sell no French wines here, sir.

Mar. Of true English growth, I assure you.

Miss Hard. Then it's odd I should not know it. We brew all sorts of wines in this house, and I have lived here these eighteen years.

Mar. Eighteen years ! Why, one would think, child, you kept the bar before you were born. How old are you ?

Miss Hard. O ! sir, I must not tell my age. They say women and music should never be dated.

Mar. To guess at this distance, you can't be much above forty (*approaching*). Yet, nearer, I don't think so much (*approaching*). By coming close to some women they look younger still ; but when we come very close indeed—(*attempting to kiss her*).

Miss Hard. Pray, sir, keep your distance. One would think you wanted to know one's age, as they do horses, by mark of mouth.

Mar. I protest, child, you use me extremely ill. If you keep me at this distance, how is it possible you and I can ever be acquainted ?

Miss Hard. And who wants to be acquainted with you ? I want no such acquaintance, not I. I'm sure you did not treat Miss Hardcastle, that was here awhile ago, in this obstropalous manner. I'll warrant me, before her you looked dashed, and kept bowing to the ground, and talked, for all the world, as if you was before a justice of peace.

Mar. (*Aside.*) Egad, she has hit it, sure enough! (*To her.*) In awe of her, child? Ha! ha! ha! A mere awkward squinting thing; no, no. I find you don't know me. I laughed and rallied her a little; but I was unwilling to be too severe. No, I could not be too severe, curse me!

Miss Hard. O! then, sir, you are a favourite, I find, among the ladies?

Mar. Yes, my dear, a great favourite. And yet hang me, I don't see what they find in me to follow. At the Ladies' Club in town I'm called their agreeable Rattle. Rattle, child, is not my real name, but one I'm known by. My name is Solomons; Mr. Solomons, my dear, at your service. (*Offering to salute her.*)

Miss Hard. Hold, sir; you are introducing me to your club, not to yourself. And you're so great a favourite there, you say?

Mar. Yes, my dear. There's Mrs. Mantrap, Lady Betty Blackleg, the Countess of Sligo, Mrs. Langhorns, old Miss Biddy Buckskin, and your humble servant, keep up the spirit of the place.

Miss Hard. Then it's a very merry place, I suppose?

Mar. Yes, as merry as cards, supper, wine, and old women can make us.

Miss Hard. And their agreeable Rattle, ha! ha! ha!

Mar. (*Aside.*) Egad! I don't quite like this chit. She looks knowing, methinks. You laugh, child?

Miss Hard. I can't but laugh, to think what time they all have for minding their work or their family.

Mar. (*Aside.*) All's well; she don't laugh at me. (*To her.*) Do you ever work, child?

Miss Hard. Ay, sure. There's not a screen or quilt in the whole house but what can bear witness to that.

Mar. Odso! then you must show me your embroidery. I embroider and draw patterns myself a little. If you want a judge of your work, you must apply to me. (*Seizing her hand.*)

Miss Hard. Ay, but the colours do not look well by candlelight. You shall see all in the morning. (*Struggling.*)

Mar. And why not now, my angel ? Such beauty fires beyond the power of resistance. — Pshaw ! the father here ! My old luck : I never nicked seven that I did not throw ames ace three times following.

[*Exit* MARLOW.

Enter HARDCASTLE, *who stands in surprise.*

Hard. So, madam. So, I find *this* is your *modest* lover. This is your humble admirer, that kept his eyes fixed on the ground, and only adored at humble distance. Kate, Kate, art thou not ashamed to deceive your father so ?

Miss Hard. Never trust me, dear papa, but he's still the modest man I first took him for ; you'll be convinced of it as well as I.

Hard. By the hand of my body, I believe his impudence is infectious ! Didn't I see him seize your hand ? Didn't I see him haul you about like a milkmaid ? And now you talk of his respect and his modesty, forsooth !

Miss Hard. But if I shortly convince you of his modesty, that he has only the faults that will pass off with time, and the virtues that will improve with age, I hope you'll forgive him.

Hard. The girl would actually make one run mad ! I tell you, I'll not be convinced. I am convinced. He has scarce been three hours in the house, and he has already encroached on all my prerogatives. You may like his impudence, and call it modesty ; but my son-in-law, madam, must have very different qualifications.

Miss Hard. Sir, I ask but this night to convince you.

Hard. You shall not have half the time, for I have thoughts of turning him out this very hour.

Miss Hard. Give me that hour then, and I hope to satisfy you.

Hard. Well, an hour let it be then. But I'll have no trifling with your father. All fair and open, do you mind me.

Miss Hard. I hope, sir, you have ever found that I considered your commands as my pride ; for your kindness is such, that my duty as yet has been inclination. *[Exeunt.*

ACT THE FOURTH

Enter HASTINGS *and* MISS NEVILLE.

Hast. You surprise me ; Sir Charles Marlow expected here this night ! Where have you had your information ?

Miss Nev. You may depend upon it. I just saw his letter to Mr. Hardcastle, in which he tells him he intends setting out a few hours after his son.

Hast. Then, my Constance, all must be completed before he arrives. He knows me ; and should he find me here, would discover my name, and perhaps my designs, to the rest of the family.

Miss Nev. The jewels, I hope, are safe ?

Hast. Yes, yes, I have sent them to Marlow, who keeps the keys of our baggage. In the meantime, I'll go to prepare matters for our elopement. I have had the 'squire's promise of a fresh pair of horses ; and if I should not see him again, will write him further directions. [*Exit.*

Miss Nev. Well ! success attend you. In the meantime I'll go and amuse my aunt with the old pretence of a violent passion for my cousin. [*Exit.*

Enter MARLOW, *followed by a* Servant.

Mar. I wonder what Hastings could mean by sending me so valuable a thing as a casket to keep for him, when he knows the only place I have is the seat of a post-coach at an inn door. Have you deposited the casket with the landlady, as I ordered you ?   Have you put it into her own hands ?

Ser. Yes, your honour.

Mar. She said she'd keep it safe, did she ?

Ser. Yes, she said she'd keep it safe enough ; she asked me how I came by it ; and she said she had a great mind to make me give an account of myself.

[*Exit* Servant.

Mar. Ha ! ha ! ha !   They're safe, however.   What an unaccountable set of beings have we got amongst ! This little bar-maid though runs in my head most strangely, and drives out the absurdities of all the rest of the family.   She's mine, she must be mine, or I'm greatly mistaken.

Enter HASTINGS.

Hast. Bless me !   I quite forgot to tell her that I intended to prepare at the bottom of the garden.   Marlow here, and in spirits too !

Mar. Give me joy, George.   Crown me, shadow me with laurels !   Well, George, after all, we modest fellows don't want for success among the women.

Hast. Some women, you mean.   But what success has your honour's modesty been crowned with now, that it grows so insolent upon us ?

Mar. Didn't you see the tempting, brisk, lovely little thing, that runs about the house with a bunch of keys to its girdle ?

Hast. Well, and what then ?

Mar. She's mine, you rogue you.   Such fire, such motion, such eyes, such lips ; but, egad ! she would not let me kiss them though.

Hast. But are you so sure, so very sure of her ?

Mar. Why, man, she talked of showing me her work above stairs, and I am to improve the pattern.

Hast. But how can you, Charles, go about to rob a woman of her honour ?

Mar. Pshaw! pshaw! We all know the honour of the bar-maid of an inn. I don't intend to rob her, take my word for it; there's nothing in this house I shan't honestly pay for.

Hast. I believe the girl has virtue.

Mar. And if she has, I should be the last man in the world that would attempt to corrupt it.

Hast. You have taken care, I hope, of the casket I sent you to lock up? Is it in safety?

Mar. Yes, yes. It's safe enough. I have taken care of it. But how could you think the seat of a post-coach at an inn door a place of safety? Ah! numskull! I have taken better precautions for you than you did for yourself——I have——

Hast. What?

Mar. I have sent it to the landlady to keep for you.

Hast. To the landlady!

Mar. The landlady.

Hast. You did?

Mar. I did. She's to be answerable for its forth-coming, you know.

Hast. Yes, she'll bring it forth with a witness.

Mar. Wasn't I right? I believe you'll allow that I acted prudently upon this occasion.

Hast. (*Aside.*) He must not see my uneasiness.

Mar. You seem a little disconcerted though, methinks. Sure nothing has happened?

Hast. No, nothing. Never was in better spirits in all my life. And so you left it with the landlady, who, no doubt, very readily undertook the charge.

Mar. Rather too readily. For she not only kept the casket, but, through her great precaution, was going to keep the messenger too. Ha! ha! ha!

Hast. He! he! he! They're safe, however.

Mar. As a guinea in a miser's purse.

Hast. (*Aside.*) So now all hopes of fortune are at an end, and we must set off without it. (*To him.*) Well, Charles, I'll leave you to your meditations on the pretty

bar-maid, and, he! he! he! may you be as successful
for yourself, as you have been for me! [*Exit.*

Mar. Thank ye, George: I ask no more. Ha!
ha! ha!

Enter HARDCASTLE.

Hard. I no longer know my own house. It's turned
all topsy-turvy. His servants have got drunk already.
I'll bear it no longer; and yet, from my respect for his
father, I'll be calm. (*To him.*) Mr. Marlow, your
servant. I'm your very humble servant. (*Bowing
low.*)

Mar. Sir, your humble servant. (*Aside.*) What's to
be the wonder now?

Hard. I believe, sir, you must be sensible, sir, that no
man alive ought to be more welcome than your father's
son, sir. I hope you think so?

Mar. I do from my soul, sir. I don't want much
entreaty. I generally make my father's son welcome
wherever he goes.

Hard. I believe you do, from my soul, sir. But
though I say nothing to your own conduct, that of your
servants is insufferable. Their manner of drinking is
setting a very bad example in this house, I assure you.

Mar. I protest, my very good sir, that is no fault of
mine. If they don't drink as they ought, they are to
blame. I ordered them not to spare the cellar. I did,
I assure you. (*To the side scene.*) Here, let one of my
servants come up. (*To him.*) My positive directions
were, that as I did not drink myself, they should make
up for my deficiencies below.

Hard. Then they had your orders for what they do?
I'm satisfied!

Mar. They had, I assure you. You shall hear from
one of themselves.

Enter Servant, *drunk*.

Mar. You, Jeremy! Come forward, sirrah! What

were my orders ? Were you not told to drink freely, and call for what you thought fit, for the good of the house ?

Hard. (*Aside.*) I begin to lose my patience.

Jer. Please your honour, liberty and Fleet Street for ever ! Though I'm but a servant, I'm as good as another man. I'll drink for no man before supper, sir, damme ! Good liquor will sit upon a good supper, but a good supper will not sit upon——hiccup——on my conscience, sir.

Mar. You see, my old friend, the fellow is as drunk as he can possibly be. I don't know what you'd have more, unless you'd have the poor devil soused in a beer-barrel.

Hard. Zounds ! he'll drive me distracted, if I contain myself any longer. Mr. Marlow—Sir ; I have submitted to your insolence for more than four hours, and I see no likelihood of its coming to an end. I'm now resolved to be master here, sir ; and I desire that you and your drunken pack may leave my house directly.

Mar. Leave your house !——Sure you jest, my good friend ! What ? when I'm doing what I can to please you.

Hard. I tell you, sir, you don't please me ; so I desire you'll leave my house.

Mar. Sure you cannot be serious ? At this time o' night, and such a night ? You only mean to banter me.

Hard. I tell you, sir, I'm serious ! and now that my passions are roused, I say this house is mine, sir ; this house is mine, and I command you to leave directly.

Mar. Ha ! ha ! ha ! A puddle in a storm. I shan't stir a step, I assure you. (*In a serious tone.*) This your house, fellow ! It's my house. This is my house. Mine, while I choose to stay. What right have you to bid me leave this house, sir ? I never met with such impudence, curse me ; never in my whole life before.

Hard. Nor I, confound me if ever I did. To come to my house, to call for what he likes, to turn me out of my own chair, to insult the family, to order his servants to get drunk, and then to tell me, " This house is mine, sir." By all that's impudent, it makes me laugh. Ha ! ha ! ha ! Pray, sir (*bantering*), as you take the house, what think you of taking the rest of the furniture ? There's a pair of silver candlesticks, and there's a fire-screen, and here's a pair of brazen-nosed bellows ; perhaps you may take a fancy to them ?

Mar. Bring me your bill, sir ; bring me your bill, and let's make no more words about it.

Hard. There are a set of prints, too. What think you of the Rake's Progress, for your own apartment ?

Mar. Bring me your bill, I say ; and I'll leave you and your infernal house directly.

Hard. Then there's a mahogany table that you may see your own face in.

Mar. My bill, I say.

Hard. I had forgot the great chair for your own particular slumbers, after a hearty meal.

Mar. Zounds ! bring me my bill, I say, and let's hear no more on't.

Hard. Young man, young man, from your father's letter to me, I was taught to expect a well-bred modest man as a visitor here, but now I find him no better than a coxcomb and a bully ; but he will be down here presently, and shall hear more of it. [*Exit.*

Mar. How's this ? Sure I have not mistaken the house. Everything looks like an inn. The servants cry, coming ; the attendance is awkward ; the bar-maid, too, to attend us. But she's here, and will further in-form me. Whither so fast, child ? A word with you.

Enter MISS HARDCASTLE.

Miss Hard. Let it be short, then. I'm in a hurry. (*Aside.*) I believe he begins to find out his mistake. But it's too soon quite to undeceive him.

Mar. Pray, child, answer me one question. What are you, and what may your business in this house be ?

Miss Hard. A relation of the family, sir.

Mar. What, a poor relation.

Miss Hard. Yes, sir. A poor relation, appointed to keep the keys, and to see that the guests want nothing in my power to give them.

Mar. That is, you act as the bar-maid of this inn.

Miss Hard. Inn! O law——what brought that in your head? One of the best families in the country keep an inn—Ha! ha! ha! old Mr. Hardcastle's house an inn!

Mar. Mr. Hardcastle's house! Is this Mr. Hardcastle's house, child?

Miss Hard. Ay, sure! Whose else should it be?

Mar. So then, all's out, and I have been damnably imposed on. O, confound my stupid head, I shall be laughed at over the whole town. I shall be stuck up in caricatura in all the print-shops. The *Dullissimo Maccaroni*. To mistake this house of all others for an inn, and my father's old friend for an innkeeper! What a swaggering puppy must he take me for! What a silly puppy do I find myself! There, again, may I be hanged, my dear, but I mistook you for the bar-maid.

Miss Hard. Dear me! dear me! I'm sure there's nothing in my *behaviour* to put me on a level with one of that stamp.

Mar. Nothing, my dear, nothing. But I was in for a list of blunders, and could not help making you a subscriber. My stupidity saw everything the wrong way. I mistook your assiduity for assurance, and your simplicity for allurement. But it's over. This house I no more show *my* face in.

Miss Hard. I hope, sir, I have done nothing to disoblige you. I'm sure I should be sorry to affront any gentleman who has been so polite, and said so many civil things to me. I'm sure I should be sorry (*pretending to cry*) if he left the family upon my account. I'm sure I should be sorry if people said anything amiss, since I have no fortune but my character.

Mar. (*Aside.*) By Heaven! she weeps. This is the

first mark of tenderness I ever had from a modest woman, and it touches me. (*To her.*) Excuse me, my lovely girl ; you are the only part of the family I leave with reluctance. But to be plain with you, the difference of our birth, fortune, and education, makes an honourable connection impossible ; and I can never harbour a thought of seducing simplicity that trusted in my honour, of bringing ruin upon one whose only fault was being too lovely.

Miss Hard. (*Aside.*) Generous man ! I now begin to admire him. (*To him.*) But I am sure my family is as good as Miss Hardcastle's ; and though I'm poor, that's no great misfortune to a contented mind ; and, until this moment, I never thought that it was bad to want a fortune.

Mar. And why now, my pretty simplicity ?

Miss Hard. Because it puts me at a distance from one that, if I had a thousand pounds, I would give it all to.

Mar. (*Aside.*) This simplicity bewitches me, so that if I stay, I'm undone. I must make one bold effort, and leave her. (*To her.*) Your partiality in my favour, my dear, touches me most sensibly : and were I to live for myself alone, I could easily fix my choice. But I owe too much to the opinion of the world, too much to the authority of a father ; so that—I can scarcely speak it— it affects me. Farewell. [*Exit.*

Miss Hard. I never knew half his merit till now. He shall not go, if I have power or art to detain him. I'll still preserve the character in which I *stooped to conquer;* but will undeceive my papa, who perhaps may laugh him out of his resolution. [*Exit.*

Enter TONY *and* MISS NEVILLE.

Tony. Ay, you may steal for yourselves the next time. I have done my duty. She has got the jewels again, that's a sure thing ; but she believes it was all a mistake of the servants.

Miss Nev. But, my dear cousin, sure you won't forsake

us in this distress ? If she in the least suspects that I am going off, I shall certainly be locked up, or sent to my aunt Pedigree's, which is ten times worse.

Tony. To be sure, aunts of all kinds are damned bad things. But what can I do ? I have got you a pair of horses that will fly like Whistle-jacket ; and I'm sure you can't say but I have courted you nicely before her face. Here she comes, we must court a bit or two more, for fear she would suspect us.

[*They retire, and seem to fondle.*

Enter MRS. HARDCASTLE.

Mrs. Hard. Well, I was greatly fluttered, to be sure. But my son tells me it was all a mistake of the servants. I shan't be easy, however, till they are fairly married, and then let her keep her own fortune. But what do I see ? fondling together, as I'm alive. I never saw Tony so sprightly before. Ah ! have I caught you, my pretty doves ? What, billing, exchanging stolen glances and broken murmurs ? Ah !

Tony. As for murmurs, mother, we grumble a little now and then, to be sure. But there's no love lost between us.

Mrs. Hard. A mere sprinkling, Tony, upon the flame, only to make it burn brighter.

Miss Nev. Cousin Tony promises to give us more of his company at home. Indeed, he shan't leave us any more. It won't leave us, cousin Tony, will it ?

Tony. O ! it's a pretty creature. No, I'd sooner leave my horse in a pound, than leave you when you smile upon one so. Your laugh makes you so becoming.

Miss Nev. Agreeable cousin ! Who can help admiring that natural humour, that pleasant, broad, red, thoughtless (*patting his cheek*)—ah ! it's a bold face.

Mrs. Hard. Pretty innocence !

Tony. I'm sure I always loved cousin Con's hazel eyes, and her pretty long fingers, that she twists this way and that over the haspicholls, like a parcel of bobbins.

Mrs. Hard. Ah! he would charm the bird from the tree. I was never so happy before. My boy takes after his father, poor Mr. Lumpkin, exactly. The jewels, my dear Con, shall be yours incontinently. You shall have them. Isn't he a sweet boy, my dear? You shall be married to-morrow, and we'll put off the rest of his education, like Dr. Drowsy's sermons, to a fitter opportunity.

Enter DIGGORY.

Dig. Where's the 'squire? I have got a letter for your worship.

Tony. Give it to my mamma. She reads all my letters first.

Dig. I had orders to deliver it into your own hands.

Tony. Who does it come from?

Dig. Your worship mun ask that o' the letter itself.

Tony. I could wish to know though (*turning the letter, and gazing on it.*)

Miss Nev. (*Aside.*) Undone! undone! A letter to him from Hastings. I know the hand. If my aunt sees it, we are ruined for ever. I'll keep her employed a little if I can. (*To* MRS. HARDCASTLE.) But I have not told you, madam, of my cousin's smart answer just now to Mr. Marlow. We so laughed.—You must know, madam.—This way a little, for he must not hear us.

[*They confer.*

Tony. (*Still gazing.*) A damned cramp piece of penmanship, as ever I saw in my life. I can read your print hand very well. But here are such handles, and shanks, and dashes, that one can scarce tell the head from the tail.—" To Anthony Lumpkin, Esquire." It's very odd, I can read the outside of my letters, where my own name is, well enough; but when I come to open it, it's all—— buzz. That's hard, very hard; for the inside of the letter is always the cream of the correspondence.

Mrs. Hard. Ha! ha! ha! Very well, very well. And so my son was too hard for the philosopher.

Miss Nev. Yes, madam ; but you must hear the rest, madam. A little more this way, or he may hear us. You'll hear how he puzzled him again.

Mrs. Hard. He seems strangely puzzled now himself, methinks.

Tony. (*Still gazing.*) A damned up and down hand, as if it was disguised in liquor.—(*Reading.*) Dear Sir,— ay, that's that. Then there's an M, and a T, and an S, but whether the next be an izzard, or an R, confound me, I cannot tell.

Mrs. Hard. What's that, my dear ? Can I give you any assistance ?

Miss Nev. Pray, aunt, let me read it. Nobody reads a cramp hand better than I. (*Twitching the letter from him.*) Do you know who it is from ?

Tony. Can't tell, except from Dick Ginger, the feeder.

Miss Nev. Ay, so it is. (*Pretending to read.*) Dear 'Squire, hoping that you're in health, as I am at this present. The gentlemen of the Shake-bag club has cut the gentlemen of Goose-green quite out of feather. The odds—um—odd battle—um—long fighting—um—here, here, it's all about cocks and fighting ; it's of no consequence ; here, put it up, put it up. (*Thrusting the crumpled letter upon him.*)

Tony. But I tell you, miss, it's of all the consequence in the world. I would not lose the rest of it for a guinea. Here, mother, do you make it out. Of no consequence ! (*Giving* Mrs. Hardcastle *the letter.*)

Mrs. Hard. How's this ?—(*Reads.*) " Dear 'Squire, I'm now waiting for Miss Neville, with a post-chaise and pair, at the bottom of the garden, but I find my horses yet unable to perform the journey. I expect you'll assist us with a pair of fresh horses, as you promised. Dispatch is necessary, as the *hag* (ay, the hag), your mother, will otherwise suspect us ! Yours, Hastings." Grant me patience. I shall run distracted ! My rage chokes me.

Miss Nev. I hope, madam, you'll suspend your resentment for a few moments, and not impute to me any impertinence, or sinister design, that belongs to another.

Mrs. Hard. (*Curtseying very low.*) Fine spoken, madam, you are most miraculously polite and engaging, and quite the very pink of courtesy and circumspection, madam. (*Changing her tone.*) And you, you great ill-fashioned oaf, with scarce sense enough to keep your mouth shut : were you, too, joined against me ? But I'll defeat all your plots in a moment. As for you, madam, since you have got a pair of fresh horses ready, it would be cruel to disappoint them. So, if you please, instead of running away with your spark, prepare, this very moment, to run off with *me*. Your old aunt Pedigree will keep you secure, I'll warrant me. You too, sir, may mount your horse, and guard us upon the way. Here, Thomas, Roger, Diggory ! I'll show you, that I wish you better than you do yourselves. [*Exit.*

Miss Nev. So now I'm completely ruined.

Tony. Ay, that's a sure thing.

Miss Nev. What better could be expected from being connected with such a stupid fool,—and after all the nods and signs I made him ?

Tony. By the laws, miss, it was your own cleverness, and not my stupidity, that did your business. You were so nice and so busy with your Shake-bags and Goose-greens, that I thought you could never be making believe.

Enter HASTINGS.

Hast. So, sir, I find by my servant, that you have shown my letter, and betrayed us. Was this well done, young gentleman ?

Tony. Here's another. Ask miss, there, who betrayed you. Ecod, it was her doing, not mine.

Enter MARLOW.

Mar. So I have been finely used here among you.

Rendered contemptible, driven into ill manners, despised, insulted, laughed at.

Tony. Here's another. We shall have old Bedlam broke loose presently.

Miss Nev. And there, sir, is the gentleman to whom we all owe every obligation.

Mar. What can I say to him, a mere boy, an idiot, whose ignorance and age are a protection?

Hast. A poor contemptible booby, that would but disgrace correction.

Miss Nev. Yet with cunning and malice enough to make himself merry with all our embarrassments.

Hast. An insensible cub.

Mar. Replete with tricks and mischief.

Tony. Baw! damme, but I'll fight you both, one after the other——with baskets.

Mar. As for him, he's below resentment. But your conduct, Mr. Hastings, requires an explanation. You knew of my mistakes, yet would not undeceive me.

Hast. Tortured as I am with my own disappointments, is this a time for explanations? It is not friendly, Mr. Marlow.

Mar. But, sir——

Miss Nev. Mr. Marlow, we never kept on your mistake till it was too late to undeceive you.

Enter Servant.

Ser. My mistress desires you'll get ready immediately, madam. The horses are putting to. Your hat and things are in the next room. We are to go thirty miles before morning.   [*Exit Servant.*

Miss Nev. Well, well: I'll come presently.

Mar. (*To* HASTINGS.) Was it well done, sir, to assist in rendering me ridiculous? To hang me out for the scorn of all my acquaintance? Depend upon it, sir, I shall expect an explanation.

Hast. Was it well done, sir, if you're upon that

subject, to deliver what I entrusted to yourself, to the
care of another, sir?

Miss Nev. Mr. Hastings! Mr. Marlow! Why will
you increase my distress by this groundless dispute?
I implore, I entreat you——

Enter Servant.

Ser. Your cloak, madam. My mistress is impatient.
                                        [*Exit* Servant.

Miss Nev. I come. Pray be pacified. If I leave you
thus, I shall die with apprehension.

Enter Servant.

Ser. Your fan, muff, and gloves, madam. The horses
are waiting.

Miss Nev. O, Mr. Marlow! if you knew what a scene
of constraint and ill-nature lies before me, I'm sure it
would convert your resentment into pity.

Mar. I'm so distracted with a variety of passions,
that I don't know what I do. Forgive me, madam.
George, forgive me. You know my hasty temper, and
should not exasperate it.

Hast. The torture of my situation is my only excuse.

Miss Nev. Well, my dear Hastings, if you have that
esteem for me that I think, that I am sure you have,
your constancy for three years will but increase the
happiness of our future connection. If——

Miss Hard. (*Within.*) Miss Neville. Constance, why
Constance, I say.

Miss Nev. I'm coming. Well, constancy, remember,
constancy is the word.   [*Exit.*

Hast. My heart! how can I support this? To be
so near happiness, and such happiness.

Mar. (*To* TONY.) You see now, young gentleman,
the effects of your folly. What might be amusement
to you, is here disappointment, and even distress.

Tony. (*From a reverie.*) Ecod, I have hit it. It's

here.   Your hands.   Yours and yours, my poor Sulky!
—My boots there, ho!—Meet me two hours hence at
the bottom of the garden; and if you don't find Tony
Lumpkin a more good-natured fellow than you thought
for, I'll give you leave to take my best horse, and Bet
Bouncer into the bargain.   Come along.   My boots,
ho!   [*Exeunt.*

ACT THE FIFTH

(SCENE *continued*.)

Enter HASTINGS *and* Servant.

Hast. You saw the old lady and Miss Neville drive off, you say ?

Ser. Yes, your honour. They went off in a post-coach, and the young 'squire went on horseback. They're thirty miles off by this time.

Hast. Then all my hopes are over.

Ser. Yes, sir. Old Sir Charles has arrived. He and the old gentleman of the house have been laughing at Mr. Marlow's mistake this half-hour. They are coming this way.

Hast. Then I must not be seen. So now to my fruit-less appointment at the bottom of the garden. This is about the time.   [*Exit.*

Enter SIR CHARLES *and* HARDCASTLE.

Hard. Ha ! ha ! ha ! The peremptory tone in which he sent forth his sublime commands !

Sir Cha. And the reserve with which I suppose he treated all your advances.

Hard. And yet he might have seen something in me above a common innkeeper, too.

Sir Cha. Yes, Dick, but he mistook you for an un-common innkeeper, ha ! ha ! ha !

Hard. Well, I'm in too good spirits to think of any-thing but joy. Yes, my dear friend, this union of our families will make our personal friendships hereditary ; and though my daughter's fortune is but small——

Sir Cha. Why, Dick, will you talk of fortune to *me?* My son is possessed of more than a competence already, and can want nothing but a good and virtuous girl to share his happiness and increase it. If they like each other, as you say they do——

Hard. If, man! I tell you they *do* like each other. My daughter as good as told me so.

Sir Cha. But girls are apt to flatter themselves, you know.

Hard. I saw him grasp her hand in the warmest manner myself ; and here he comes to put you out of your *ifs*, I warrant him.

Enter MARLOW.

Mar. I come, sir, once more, to ask pardon for my strange conduct. I can scarce reflect on my insolence without confusion.

Hard. Tut, boy, a trifle! You take it too gravely. An hour or two's laughing with my daughter will set all to rights again. She'll never like you the worse for it.

Mar. Sir, I shall be always proud of her approbation.

Hard. Approbation is but a cold word, Mr. Marlow ; if I am not deceived, you have something more than approbation thereabouts. You take me?

Mar. Really, sir, I have not that happiness.

Hard. Come, boy, I'm an old fellow, and know what's what as well as you that are younger. I know what has passed between you ; but mum.

Mar. Sure, sir, nothing has passed between us but the most profound respect on my side, and the most distant reserve on hers. You don't think, sir, that my impudence has been passed upon all the rest of the family.

Hard. Impudence! No, I don't say that—not quite impudence—though girls like to be played with, and rumpled a little too, sometimes. But she has told no tales, I assure you.

Mar. I never gave her the slightest cause.

Hard. Well, well, I like modesty in its place well enough. But this is over-acting, young gentleman. You may be open. Your father and I will like you all the better for it.

Mar. May I die, sir, if I ever——

Hard. I tell you, she don't dislike you; and as I'm sure you like her——

Mar. Dear sir—I protest, sir——

Hard. I see no reason why you should not be joined as fast as the parson can tie you.

Mar. But hear me, sir——

Hard. Your father approves the match, I admire it; every moment's delay will be doing mischief. So——

Mar. But why won't you hear me? By all that's just and true, I never gave Miss Hardcastle the slightest mark of my attachment, or even the most distant hint to suspect me of affection. We had but one interview, and that was formal, modest, and uninteresting.

Hard. (*Aside.*) This fellow's formal modest impudence is beyond bearing.

Sir Cha. And you never grasped her hand, or made any protestations?

Mar. As Heaven is my witness, I came down in obedience to your commands. I saw the lady without emotion, and parted without reluctance. I hope you'll exact no further proofs of my duty, nor prevent me from leaving a house in which I suffer so many mortifications. [*Exit.*

Sir Cha. I'm astonished at the air of sincerity with which he parted.

Hard. And I'm astonished at the deliberate intrepidity of his assurance.

Sir Cha. I dare pledge my life and honour upon his truth.

Hard. Here comes my daughter, and I would stake my happiness upon her veracity.

Enter MISS HARDCASTLE.

Hard. Kate, come hither, child. Answer us sincerely and without reserve : has Mr. Marlow made you any professions of love and affection ?

Miss Hard. The question is very abrupt, sir. But since you require unreserved sincerity, I think he has.

Hard. (*To* SIR CHARLES.) You see.

Sir Cha. And pray, madam, have you and my son had more than one interview ?

Miss Hard. Yes, sir, several.

Hard. (*To* SIR CHARLES.) You see.

Sir Cha. But did he profess any attachment ?

Miss Hard. A lasting one.

Sir Cha. Did he talk of love ?

Miss Hard. Much, sir.

Sir Cha. Amazing ! And all this formally ?

Miss Hard. Formally.

Hard. Now, my friend, I hope you are satisfied.

Sir Cha. And how did he behave, madam ?

Miss Hard. As most profest admirers do : said some civil things of my face, talked much of his want of merit, and the greatness of mine ; mentioned his heart, gave a short tragedy speech, and ended with pretended rapture.

Sir Cha. Now I'm perfectly convinced, indeed. I know his conversation among women to be modest and submissive : this forward canting ranting manner by no means describes him ; and, I am confident, he never sat for the picture.

Miss Hard. Then, what, sir, if I should convince you to your face of my sincerity ? If you and my papa, in about half an hour, will place yourselves behind that screen, you shall hear him declare his passion to me in person.

Sir Cha. Agreed. And if I find him what you describe, all my happiness in him must have an end.   [*Exit.*

Miss Hard. And if you don't find him what I describe —I fear my happiness must never have a beginning.
                              [*Exeunt.*

SCENE *changes to the back of the Garden.*

Enter HASTINGS.

Hast. What an idiot am I, to wait here for a fellow who probably takes a delight in mortifying me. He never intended to be punctual, and I'll wait no longer. What do I see ? It is he ! and perhaps with news of my Constance.

Enter TONY, *booted and spattered.*

Hast. My honest 'squire ! I now find you a man of your word. This looks like friendship.

Tony. Ay, I'm your friend, and the best friend you have in the world, if you knew but all. This riding by night, by the bye, is cursedly tiresome. It has shook me worse than the basket of a stage-coach.

Hast. But how ? where did you leave your fellow-travellers ? Are they in safety ? Are they housed ?

Tony. Five-and-twenty miles in two hours and a half is no such bad driving. The poor beasts have smoked for it : rabbit me, but I'd rather ride forty miles after a fox than ten with such varment.

Hast. Well, but where have you left the ladies ? I die with impatience.

Tony. Left them ! Why, where should I leave them but where I found them ?

Hast. This is a riddle.

Tony. Riddle me this then. What's that goes round the house, and round the house, and never touches the house ?

Hast. I'm still astray.

Tony. Why, that's it, mon. I have led them astray. By jingo, there's not a pond or a slough within five miles of the place but they can tell the taste of.

Hast. Ha! ha! ha! I understand: you took them in a round, while they supposed themselves going forward, and so you have at last brought them home again.

Tony. You shall hear. I first took them down Feather-bed Lane, where we stuck fast in the mud. I then rattled them crack over the stones of Up-and-down Hill. I then introduced them to the gibbet on Heavy-tree Heath; and from that, with a circumbendibus, I fairly lodged them in the horse-pond at the bottom of the garden.

Hast. But no accident, I hope?

Tony. No, no. Only mother is confoundedly frightened. She thinks herself forty miles off. She's sick of the journey; and the cattle can scarce crawl. So if your own horses be ready, you may whip off with cousin, and I'll be bound that no soul here can budge a foot to follow you.

Hast. My dear friend, how can I be grateful?

Tony. Ay, now it's dear friend, noble 'squire. Just now, it was all idiot, cub, and run me through the guts. Damn *your* way of fighting, I say. After we take a knock in this part of the country, we kiss and be friends. But if you had run me through the guts, then I should be dead, and you might go kiss the hangman.

Hast. The rebuke is just. But I must hasten to relieve Miss Neville: if you keep the old lady employed, I promise to take care of the young one. [*Exit* HASTINGS.

Tony. Never fear me. Here she comes. Vanish. She's got from the pond, and draggled up to the waist like a mermaid.

Enter MRS. HARDCASTLE.

Mrs. Hard. Oh, Tony, I'm killed! Shook! Battered to death. I shall never survive it. That last jolt that laid us against the quickset hedge, has done my business.

Tony. Alack, mamma, it was all your own fault. You would be for running away by night, without knowing one inch of the way.

Mrs. Hard. I wish we were at home again. I never met so many accidents in so short a journey. Drenched in the mud, overturned in a ditch, stuck fast in a slough, jolted to a jelly, and at last to lose our way. Whereabouts do you think we are, Tony?

Tony. By my guess we should come upon Crackskull Common, about forty miles from home.

Mrs. Hard. O lud! O lud! The most notorious spot in all the country. We only want a robbery to make a complete night on't.

Tony. Don't be afraid, mamma, don't be afraid. Two of the five that kept here are hanged, and the other three may not find us. Don't be afraid.—Is that a man that's galloping behind us? No; it's only a tree. —Don't be afraid.

Mrs. Hard. The fright will certainly kill me.

Tony. Do you see anything like a black hat moving behind the thicket?

Mrs. Hard. Oh, death!

Tony. No; it's only a cow. Don't be afraid, mamma; don't be afraid.

Mrs. Hard. As I'm alive, Tony, I see a man coming towards us. Ah! I'm sure on't. If he perceives us, we are undone.

Tony. (*Aside.*) Father-in-law, by all that's unlucky, come to take one of his night walks. (*To her.*) Ah, it's a highwayman with pistols as long as my arm. A damned ill-looking fellow.

Mrs. Hard. Good Heaven defend us! He approaches.

Tony. Do you hide yourself in that thicket, and leave me to manage him. If there be any danger, I'll cough, and cry hem. When I cough, be sure to keep close. (MRS. HARDCASTLE *hides behind a tree in the back scene.*)

Enter HARDCASTLE.

Hard. I'm mistaken, or I heard voices of people in want of help. Oh, Tony! is that you? I did not expect you so soon back. Are your mother and her charge in safety?

Tony. Very safe, sir, at my aunt Pedigree's. Hem.

Mrs. Hard. (*From behind.*) Ah, death! I find there's danger.

Hard. Forty miles in three hours; sure that's too much, my youngster.

Tony. Stout horses and willing minds make short journeys, as they say. Hem.

Mrs. Hard. (*From behind.*) Sure he'll do the dear boy no harm.

Hard. But I heard a voice here; I should be glad to know from whence it came.

Tony. It was I, sir, talking to myself, sir. I was saying that forty miles in four hours was very good going. Hem. As to be sure it was. Hem. I have got a sort of cold by being out in the air. We'll go in, if you please. Hem.

Hard. But if you talked to yourself you did not answer yourself. I'm certain I heard two voices, and am resolved (*raising his voice*) to find the other out.

Mrs. Hard. (*From behind.*) Oh! he's coming to find me out. Oh!

Tony. What need you go, sir, if I tell you? Hem. I'll lay down my life for the truth—hem—I'll tell you all, sir. (*Detaining him.*)

Hard. I tell you I will not be detained. I insist on seeing. It's in vain to expect I'll believe you.

Mrs. Hard. (*Running forward from behind.*) O lud! he'll murder my poor boy, my darling! Here, good gentleman, whet your rage upon me. Take my money, my life, but spare that young gentleman; spare my child, if you have any mercy.

Hard. My wife, as I'm a Christian. From whence can she come ? or what does she mean ?

Mrs. Hard. (*Kneeling.*) Take compassion on us, good Mr. Highwayman. Take our money, our watches, all we have, but spare our lives. We will never bring you to justice ; indeed we won't, good Mr. Highwayman.

Hard. I believe the woman's out of her senses. What, Dorothy, don't you know *me* ?

Mrs. Hard. Mr. Hardcastle, as I'm alive ! My fears blinded me. But who, my dear, could have expected to meet you here, in this frightful place, so far from home ? What has brought you to follow us ?

Hard. Sure, Dorothy, you have not lost your wits ? So far from home, when you are within forty yards of your own door ! (*To him.*) This is one of your old tricks, you graceless rogue, you. (*To her.*) Don't you know the gate, and the mulberry-tree ; and don't you remember the horse-pond, my dear ?

Mrs. Hard. Yes, I shall remember the horse-pond as long as I live ; I have caught my death in it. (*To* Tony.) And is it to you, you graceless varlet, I owe all this ? I'll teach you to abuse your mother, I will.

Tony. Ecod, mother, all the parish says you have spoiled me, and so you may take the fruits on't.

Mrs. Hard. I'll spoil you, I will.

[*Follows him off the stage. Exit.*

Hard. There's morality, however, in his reply. [*Exit.*

Enter HASTINGS *and* MISS NEVILLE.

Hast. My dear Constance, why will you deliberate thus ? If we delay a moment, all is lost for ever. Pluck up a little resolution, and we shall soon be out of the reach of her malignity.

Miss Nev. I find it impossible. My spirits are so sunk with the agitations I have suffered, that I am unable to face any new danger. Two or three years' patience will at last crown us with happiness.

Hast. Such a tedious delay is worse than inconstancy. Let us fly, my charmer. Let us date our happiness from this very moment. Perish fortune ! Love and content will increase what we possess beyond a monarch's revenue. Let me prevail !

Miss Nev. No, Mr. Hastings, no. Prudence once more comes to my relief, and I will obey its dictates. In the moment of passion fortune may be despised, but it ever produces a lasting repentance. I'm resolved to apply to Mr. Hardcastle's compassion and justice for redress.

Hast. But though he had the will, he has not the power to relieve you.

Miss Nev. But he has influence, and upon that I am resolved to rely.

Hast. I have no hopes. But since you persist, I must reluctantly obey you. [*Exeunt.*

Scene *changes.*

Enter Sir Charles *and* Miss Hardcastle.

Sir Cha. What a situation am I in ! If what you say appears, I shall then find a guilty son. If what he says be true, I shall then lose one that, of all others, I most wished for a daughter.

Miss Hard. I am proud of your approbation, and to show I merit it, if you place yourselves as I directed, you shall hear his explicit declaration. But he comes.

Sir Cha. I'll to your father, and keep him to the appointment. [*Exit* Sir Charles.

Enter Marlow.

Mar. Though prepared for setting out, I come once more to take leave ; nor did I, till this moment, know the pain I feel in the separation.

Miss Hard. (*In her own natural manner.*) I believe

these sufferings cannot be very great, sir, which you can so easily remove. A day or two longer, perhaps, might lessen your uneasiness, by showing the little value of what you now think proper to regret.

Mar. (*Aside.*) This girl every moment improves upon me. (*To her.*) It must not be, madam, I have already trifled too long with my heart. My very pride begins to submit to my passion. The disparity of education and fortune, the anger of a parent, and the contempt of my equals, begin to lose their weight; and nothing can restore me to myself but this painful effort of resolution.

Miss Hard. Then go, sir: I'll urge nothing more to detain you. Though my family be as good as hers you came down to visit, and my education, I hope, not inferior, what are these advantages without equal affluence? I must remain contented with the slight approbation of imputed merit; I must have only the mockery of your addresses, while all your serious aims are fixed on fortune.

Enter HARDCASTLE *and* SIR CHARLES *from behind.*

Sir Cha. Here, behind this screen.

Hard. Ay, ay; make no noise. I'll engage my Kate covers him with confusion at last.

Mar. By heavens, madam! fortune was ever my smallest consideration. Your beauty at first caught my eye; for who could see that without emotion? But every moment that I converse with you steals in some new grace, heightens the picture, and gives it stronger expression. What at first seemed rustic plainness, now appears refined simplicity. What seemed forward assurance, now strikes me as the result of courageous innocence and conscious virtue.

Sir Cha. What can it mean? He amazes me!

Hard. I told you how it would be. Hush!

Mar. I am now determined to stay, madam; and I

have too good an opinion of my father's discernment, when he sees you, to doubt his approbation.

Miss Hard. No, Mr. Marlow, I will not, cannot detain you. Do you think I could suffer a connection in which there is the smallest room for repentance? Do you think I would take the mean advantage of a transient passion, to load you with confusion? Do you think I could ever relish that happiness which was acquired by lessening yours?

Mar. By all that's good, I can have no happiness but what's in your power to grant me! Nor shall I ever feel repentance but in not having seen your merits before. I will stay even contrary to your wishes; and though you should persist to shun me, I will make my respectful assiduities atone for the levity of my past conduct.

Miss Hard. Sir, I must entreat you'll desist. As our acquaintance began, so let it end, in indifference. I might have given an hour or two to levity; but seriously, Mr. Marlow, do you think I could ever submit to a connection where I must appear mercenary, and you imprudent? Do you think I could ever catch at the confident addresses of a secure admirer?

Mar. (*Kneeling.*) Does this look like security? Does this look like confidence? No, madam, every moment that shows me your merit, only serves to increase my diffidence and confusion. Here let me continue——

Sir Cha. I can hold it no longer. Charles, Charles, how hast thou deceived me! Is this your indifference, your uninteresting conversation?

Hard. Your cold contempt; your formal interview! What have you to say now?

Mar. That I'm all amazement! What can it mean?

Hard. It means that you can say and unsay things at pleasure: that you can address a lady in private, and deny it in public: that you have one story for us, and another for my daughter.

Mar. Daughter!—This lady your daughter?

Hard. Yes, sir; my only daughter; my Kate; whose else should she be?

Mar. Oh, the devil!

Miss Hard. Yes, sir, that very identical tall squinting lady you were pleased to take me for (*curtseying*); she that you addressed as the mild, modest, sentimental man of gravity, and the bold, forward, agreeable Rattle of the Ladies' Club. Ha! ha! ha!

Mar. Zounds! there's no bearing this; it's worse than death!

Miss Hard. In which of your characters, sir, will you give us leave to address you? As the faltering gentleman, with looks on the ground, that speaks just to be heard, and hates hypocrisy; or the loud confident creature, that keeps it up with Mrs. Mantrap, and old Miss Biddy Buckskin, till three in the morning? Ha! ha! ha!

Mar. O, curse on my noisy head. I never attempted to be impudent yet, that I was not taken down. I must be gone.

Hard. By the hand of my body, but you shall not. I see it was all a mistake, and I am rejoiced to find it. You shall not, sir, I tell you. I know she'll forgive you. Won't you forgive him, Kate? We'll all forgive you. Take courage, man. (*They retire, she tormenting him, to the back scene.*)

Enter MRS. HARDCASTLE *and* TONY.

Mrs. Hard. So, so, they're gone off. Let them go, I care not.

Hard. Who gone?

Mrs. Hard. My dutiful niece and her gentleman, Mr. Hastings, from town. He who came down with our modest visitor here.

Sir Cha. Who, my honest George Hastings? As worthy a fellow as lives, and the girl could not have made a more prudent choice.

Hard. Then, by the hand of my body, I'm proud of the connection.

Mrs. Hard. Well, if he has taken away the lady, he has not taken her fortune ; that remains in this family to console us for her loss.

Hard. Sure, Dorothy, you would not be so mercenary ?

Mrs. Hard. Ay, that's my affair, not yours.

Hard. But you know if your son, when of age, refuses to marry his cousin, her whole fortune is then at her own disposal.

Mrs. Hard. Ay, but he's not of age, and she has not thought proper to wait for his refusal.

Enter HASTINGS *and* MISS NEVILLE.

Mrs. Hard. (*Aside.*) What, returned so soon ! I begin not to like it.

Hast. (*To* HARDCASTLE.) For my late attempt to fly off with your niece let my present confusion be my punishment. We are now come back, to appeal from your justice to your humanity. By her father's consent, I first paid her my addresses, and our passions were first founded in duty.

Miss Nev. Since his death, I have been obliged to stoop to dissimulation to avoid oppression. In an hour of levity, I was ready to give up my fortune to secure my choice. But I am now recovered from the delusion, and hope from your tenderness what is denied me from a nearer connection.

Mrs. Hard. Pshaw, pshaw ! this is all but the whining end of a modern novel.

Hard. Be it what it will, I'm glad they're come back to reclaim their due. Come hither, Tony, boy. Do you refuse this lady's hand whom I now offer you ?

Tony. What signifies my refusing ? You know I can't refuse her till I'm of age, father.

Hard. While I thought concealing your age, boy, was likely to conduce to your improvement, I concurred with your mother's desire to keep it secret. But since I find she turns it to a wrong use, I must now declare you have been of age these three months.

Tony. Of age! Am I of age, father?

Hard. Above three months.

Tony. Then you'll see the first use I'll make of my liberty. (*Taking* Miss Neville's *hand.*) Witness all men by these presents, that I, Anthony Lumpkin, Esquire, of BLANK place, refuse you, Constantia Neville, spinster, of no place at all, for my true and lawful wife. So Constance Neville may marry whom she pleases, and Tony Lumpkin is his own man again.

Sir Cha. O brave 'squire!

Hast. My worthy friend!

Mrs. Hard. My undutiful offspring!

Mar. Joy, my dear George! I give you joy sincerely. And could I prevail upon my little tyrant here to be less arbitrary, I should be the happiest man alive, if you would return me the favour.

Hast. (*To* Miss Hardcastle.) Come, madam, you are now driven to the very last scene of all your contrivances. I know you like him, I'm sure he loves you, and you must and shall have him.

Hard. (*Joining their hands.*) And I say so too. And, Mr. Marlow, if she makes as good a wife as she has a daughter, I don't believe you'll ever repent your bargain. So now to supper. To-morrow we shall gather all the poor of the parish about us, and the mistakes of the night shall be crowned with a merry morning. So, boy, take her; and as you have been mistaken in the mistress, my wish is, that you may never be mistaken in the wife.

[*Exeunt Omnes.*

EPILOGUE

Well, having stooped to conquer with success,
And gained a husband without aid from dress,
Still, as a bar-maid, I could wish it too,
As I have conquered him to conquer you :
And let me say, for all your resolution,
That pretty bar-maids have done execution.
Our life is all a play, composed to please,
" We have our exits and our entrances."
The first act shows the simple country maid,
Harmless and young, of everything afraid ;
Blushes when hired, and with unmeaning action,
" I hopes as how to give you satisfaction."
Her second act displays a livelier scene—
The unblushing bar-maid of a country inn,
Who whisks about the house, at market caters,
Talks loud, coquets the guests, and scolds the waiters.
Next the scene shifts to town, and there she soars,
The chop-house toast of ogling *connoisseurs*.
On 'squires and cits she there displays her arts,
And on the gridiron broils her lovers' heart—
And as she smiles, her triumphs to complete,
E'en common-councilmen forget to eat.
The fourth act shows her wedded to the 'squire,
And madam now begins to hold it higher ;
Pretends to taste, at operas cries caro !
And quits her Nancy Dawson, for Che Faro :
Doats upon dancing, and in all her pride
Swims round the room, the Heinel of Cheapside :
Ogles and leers with artificial skill,
Till, having lost in age the power to kill,
She sits all night at cards, and ogles at spadille.

Such, through our lives the eventful history—
The fifth and last act still remains for me.
The bar-maid now for your protection prays,
Turns female barrister, and pleads for Bayes.

EPILOGUE

To be Spoken in the Character of Tony Lumpkin

BY J. CRADOCK, ESQ.

WELL—now all's ended—and my comrades gone,
Pray what becomes of " mother's nonly son " ?
A hopeful blade !—in town I'll fix my station,
And try to make a bluster in the nation ;
As for my cousin Neville, I renounce her,
Off—in a crack—I'll carry big Bet Bouncer.

Why should not I in the great world appear ?
I soon shall have a thousand pounds a year !
No matter what a man may here inherit,
In London—'gad, they've some regard to spirit.
I see the horses prancing up the streets,
And big Bet Bouncer bobs to all she meets ;
Then hoiks to jigs and pastimes ev'ry night—
Not to the plays—they say it a'n't polite ;
To Sadler's-Well perhaps, or operas go,
And once by chance, to the roratorio.
Thus here and there, for ever up and down,
We'll set the fashions too to half the town ;
And then at auctions—money ne'er regard,
Buy pictures like the great, ten pounds a yard :
Zounds, we shall make these London gentry say,
We know what's damned genteel as well as they.

THE GOOD-NATURED MAN

A COMEDY

AS PERFORMED AT THE THEATRE ROYAL,
COVENT GARDEN

[1768]

PREFACE

WHEN I undertook to write a comedy, I confess I was strongly prepossessed in favour of the poets of the last age, and strove to imitate them. The term "genteel comedy" was then unknown amongst us, and little more was desired by an audience than nature and humour, in whatever walks of life they were most conspicuous. The author of the following scenes never imagined that more would be expected of him, and therefore to delineate character has been his principal aim. Those who know anything of composition, are sensible that, in pursuing humour, it will sometimes lead us into the recesses of the mean ; I was even tempted to look for it in the master of a spunging-house ; but in deference to the public taste, grown of late, perhaps, too delicate, the scene of the bailiffs was retrenched in the representation. In deference also to the judgment of a few friends, who think in a particular way, the scene is here restored. The author submits it to the reader in his closet ; and hopes that too much refinement will not banish humour and character from ours, as it has already done from the French theatre. Indeed, the French comedy is now become so very elevated and sentimental, that it has not only banished humour and Molière from the stage, but it has banished all spectators too.

Upon the whole, the author returns his thanks to the public for the favourable reception which *The Good-Natured Man* has met with ; and to Mr. Colman in particular, for his kindness to it. It may not also be improper to assure any who shall hereafter write for the theatre, that merit, or supposed merit, will ever be a sufficient passport to his protection.

PROLOGUE

WRITTEN BY DR. JOHNSON ; SPOKEN BY MR. BENSLEY

PRESSED by the load of life, the weary mind
Surveys the general toil of human kind ;
With cool submission joins the lab'ring train,
And social sorrow loses half its pain :
Our anxious bard, without complaint, may share
This bustling season's epidemic care,
Like Cæsar's pilot, dignified by fate,
Tost in one common storm with all the great ;
Distrest alike, the statesman and the wit,
When one a borough courts, and one the pit,
The busy candidates for power and fame
Have hopes, and fears, and wishes, just the same ;
Disabled both to combat, or to fly,
Must hear all taunts, and hear without reply.
Unchecked on both, loud rabbles vent their rage,
As mongrels bay the lion in a cage.
Th' offended burgess hoards his angry tale
For that blest year when all that vote may rail ;
Their schemes of spite the poet's foes dismiss
Till that glad night when all that hate may hiss.
" This day the powdered curls and golden coat,"
Says swelling Crispin, " begged a cobbler's vote."
" This night our wit," the pert apprentice cries,
" Lies at my feet—I hiss him, and he dies."
The great, 'tis true, can charm the electing tribe ;
The bard may supplicate, but cannot bribe.
Yet judged by those whose voices ne'er were sold,
He feels no want of ill-persuading gold ;
But confident of praise, if praise be due,
Trusts without fear, to merit, and to you.

DRAMATIS PERSONÆ

MEN

MR. HONEYWOOD	*Mr. Powell.*
CROAKER.	*Mr. Shuter.*
LOFTY	*Mr. Woodward.*
SIR WILLIAM HONEYWOOD .	*Mr. Clarke.*
LEONTINE	*Mr. Bensley.*
JARVIS	*Mr. Dunstall.*
BUTLER	*Mr. Cushing.*
BAILIFF	*Mr. R. Smith.*
DUBARDIEU	*Mr. Holtom.*
POSTBOY	*Mr. Quick.*

WOMEN

MISS RICHLAND	*Mrs. Bulkley.*
OLIVIA	*Mrs. Mattocks.*
MRS. CROAKER	*Mrs. Pitt.*
GARNET	*Mrs. Green.*
LANDLADY	*Mrs. White.*

SCENE.—*London.*

THE GOOD-NATURED MAN

ACT THE FIRST

Scene—*An Apartment in Young* Honeywood's *House.*

Enter Sir William Honeywood *and* Jarvis.

Sir Wil. Good Jarvis, make no apologies for this honest bluntness. Fidelity, like yours, is the best excuse for every freedom.

Jar. I can't help being blunt, and being very angry too, when I hear you talk of disinheriting so good, so worthy a young gentleman as your nephew, my master. All the world loves him.

Sir Wil. Say rather, that he loves all the world; that is his fault.

Jar. I am sure there is no part of it more dear to him than you are, though he has not seen you since he was a child.

Sir Wil. What signifies his affection to me; or how can I be proud of a place in a heart, where every sharper and coxcomb find an easy entrance?

Jar. I grant you that he is rather too good-natured; that he's too much every man's man; that he laughs this minute with one, and cries the next with another: but whose instructions may he thank for all this?

Sir Wil. Not mine, sure? My letters to him during

my employment in Italy taught him only that philosophy which might prevent, not defend his errors.

Jar. Faith, begging your honour's pardon, I'm sorry they taught him any philosophy at all; it has only served to spoil him. This same philosophy is a good horse in the stable, but an arrant jade on a journey. For my own part, whenever I hear him mention the name on't, I'm always sure he's going to play the fool.

Sir Wil. Don't let us ascribe his faults to his philosophy, I entreat you. No, Jarvis, his good-nature arises rather from his fears of offending the importunate, than his desire of making the deserving happy.

Jar. What it rises from, I don't know. But, to be sure, everybody has it, that asks it.

Sir Wil. Ay, or that does not ask it. I have been now for some time a concealed spectator of his follies, and find them as boundless as his dissipation.

Jar. And yet, faith, he has some fine name or other for them all. He calls his extravagance, generosity; and his trusting everybody, universal benevolence. It was but last week he went security for a fellow whose face he scarce knew, and that he called an act of exalted mu—mu—munificence; ay, that was the name he gave it.

Sir Wil. And upon that I proceed, as my last effort, though with very little hopes to reclaim him. That very fellow has just absconded, and I have taken up the security. Now, my intention is to involve him in fictitious distress, before he has plunged himself into real calamity: to arrest him for that very debt; to clap an officer upon him, and then let him see which of his friends will come to his relief.

Jar. Well, if I could but any way see him thoroughly vexed, every groan of his would be music to me; yet, faith, I believe it impossible. I have tried to fret him myself every morning these three years; but, instead of being angry, he sits as calmly to hear me scold, as he does to his hair-dresser.

Sir Wil. We must try him once more, however, and

I'll go this instant to put my scheme into execution : and I don't despair of succeeding, as, by your means, I can have frequent opportunities of being about him without being known. What a pity it is, Jarvis, that any man's goodwill to others should produce so much neglect of himself, as to require correction ! Yet we must touch his weaknesses with a delicate hand. There are some faults so nearly allied to excellence, that we can scarce weed out the vice without eradicating the virtue. [*Exit.*

Jar. Well, go thy ways, Sir William Honeywood. It is not without reason that the world allows thee to be the best of men. But here comes his hopeful nephew ; the strange, good-natured, foolish, open-hearted—And yet, all his faults are such that one loves him still the better for them.

Enter HONEYWOOD.

Hon. Well, Jarvis, what messages from my friends this morning ?

Jar. You have no friends.

Hon. Well ; from my acquaintance then ?

Jar. (*Pulling out bills.*) A few of our usual cards of compliment, that's all. This bill from your tailor ; this from your mercer ; and this from the little broker in Crooked Lane. He says he has been at a great deal of trouble to get back the money you borrowed.

Hon. That I don't know ; but I'm sure we were at a great deal of trouble in getting him to lend it.

Jar. He has lost all patience.

Hon. Then he has lost a very good thing.

Jar. There's that ten guineas you were sending to the poor gentleman and his children in the Fleet. I believe that would stop his mouth for a while at least.

Hon. Ay, Jarvis, but what will fill their mouths in the meantime ? Must I be cruel, because he happens to be importunate ; and, to relieve his avarice, leave them to insupportable distress ?

Jar. 'Sdeath ! Sir, the question now is how to relieve yourself ; yourself.—Haven't I reason to be out of my senses, when I see things going at sixes and sevens ?

Hon. Whatever reason you may have for being out of your senses, I hope you'll allow that I'm not quite unreasonable for continuing in mine.

Jar. You are the only man alive in your present situation that could do so. Everything upon the waste. There's Miss Richland and her fine fortune gone already, and upon the point of being given to your rival——

Hon. I'm no man's rival.

Jar. Your uncle in Italy preparing to disinherit you ; your own fortune almost spent ; and nothing but pressing creditors, false friends, and a pack of drunken servants that your kindness has made unfit for any other family.

Hon. Then they have the more occasion for being in mine.

Jar. Soh ! What will you have done with him that I caught stealing your plate in the pantry ? In the fact ; I caught him in the fact.

Hon. In the fact ? If so, I really think that we should pay him his wages and turn him off.

Jar. He shall be turned off at Tyburn, the dog ; we'll hang him, if it be only to frighten the rest of the family.

Hon. No, Jarvis ; it's enough that we have lost what he has stolen ; let us not add to it the loss of a fellow-creature !

Jar. Very fine ! well, here was the footman just now, to complain of the butler : he says he does most work, and ought to have most wages.

Hon. That's but just ; though perhaps here comes the butler to complain of the footman.

Jar. Ay, it's the way with them all, from the scullion to the privy-councillor. If they have a bad master, they keep quarrelling with him ; if they have a good master, they keep quarrelling with one another.

Enter Butler, *drunk.*

But. Sir, I'll not stay in the family with Jonathan ; you must part with him, or part with me ; that's the ex—ex—exposition of the matter, sir.

Hon. Full and explicit enough. But what's his fault, good Philip ?

But. Sir, he's given to drinking, sir, and I shall have my morals corrupted by keeping such company.

Hon. Ha ! ha ! he has such a diverting way——

Jar. Oh, quite amusing.

But. I find my wine's a-going, sir ; and liquors don't go without mouths, sir ; I hate a drunkard, sir.

Hon. Well, well, Philip, I'll hear you upon that another time ; so go to bed now.

Jar. To bed ! let him go to the devil.

But. Begging your honour's pardon, and begging your pardon, master Jarvis, I'll not go to bed, nor to the devil neither. I have enough to do to mind my cellar. I forgot, your honour, Mr. Croaker is below. I came on purpose to tell you.

Hon. Why didn't you show him up, blockhead ?

But. Show him up, sir ! With all my heart, sir. Up or down, all's one to me. [*Exit.*

Jar. Ay, we have one or other of that family in this house from morning till night. He comes on the old affair, I suppose. The match between his son that's just returned from Paris, and Miss Richland, the young lady he's guardian to.

Hon. Perhaps so. Mr. Croaker, knowing my friend-ship for the young lady, has got it into his head that I can persuade her to what I please.

Jar. Ah ! if you loved yourself but half as well as she loves you, we should soon see a marriage that would set all things to rights again.

Hon. Love me ! Sure, Jarvis, you dream. No, no ; her intimacy with me never amounted to more than mere friendship—mere friendship. That she is the most lovely woman that ever warmed the human heart with desire, I own. But never let me harbour a thought of making her unhappy, by a connection with one so unworthy her merits as I am. No, Jarvis, it shall be my study to serve her, even in spite of my wishes ; and to secure her happiness, though it destroys my own.

Jar. Was ever the like ? I want patience.

Hon. Besides, Jarvis, though I could obtain Miss Richland's consent, do you think I could succeed with her guardian, or Mrs. Croaker, his wife ; who, though both very fine in their way, are yet a little opposite in their dispositions, you know ?

Jar. Opposite enough, Heaven knows ! the very reverse of each other : she, all laugh and no joke ; he, always complaining and never sorrowful ; a fretful poor soul, that has a new distress for every hour in the four-and-twenty——

Hon. Hush, hush, he's coming up, he'll hear you.

Jar. One whose voice is a passing-bell——

Hon. Well, well ; go, do.

Jar. A raven that bodes nothing but mischief ; a coffin and cross-bones ; a bundle of rue ; a sprig of deadly night-shade ; a—(HONEYWOOD, *stopping his mouth, at last pushes him off.*) [*Exit* JARVIS.

Hon. I must own, my old monitor is not entirely wrong. There is something in my friend Croaker's conversation that entirely depresses me. His very mirth is quite an antidote to all gaiety, and his appearance has a stronger effect on my spirits than an undertaker's shop.—Mr. Croaker, this is such a satisfaction——

Enter CROAKER.

Cro. A pleasant morning to Mr. Honeywood, and many of them. How is this ! you look most shockingly to-day, my dear friend. I hope this weather does not affect your spirits. To be sure, if this weather continues —I say nothing—But God send we be all better this day three months !

Hon. I heartily concur in the wish, though, I own, not in your apprehensions.

Cro. Maybe not. Indeed, what signifies what weather we have in a country going to ruin like ours? Taxes rising and trade falling. Money flying out of the kingdom, and Jesuits swarming into it. I know at this time no less than a hundred and twenty-seven Jesuits between Charing Cross and Temple Bar.

Hon. The Jesuits will scarce pervert you or me, I should hope.

Cro. Maybe not. Indeed, what signifies whom they pervert in a country that has scarce any religion to lose? I'm only afraid for our wives and daughters.

Hon. I have no apprehensions for the ladies, I assure you.

Cro. Maybe not. Indeed, what signifies whether they be perverted or no? The women in my time were good for something. I have seen a lady drest from top to toe in her own manufactures formerly. But nowadays the devil a thing of their own manufacture's about them, except their faces.

Hon. But, however these faults may be practised abroad, you don't find them at home, either with Mrs. Croaker, Olivia, or Miss Richland.

Cro. The best of them will never be canonized for a saint when she's dead. By the bye, my dear friend, I don't find this match between Miss Richland and my son much relished, either by one side or t'other.

Hon. I thought otherwise.

Cro. Ah, Mr. Honeywood, a little of your fine serious advice to the young lady might go far: I know she has a very exalted opinion of your understanding.

Hon. But would not that be usurping an authority that more properly belongs to yourself?

Cro. My dear friend, you know but little of my authority at home. People think, indeed, because they see me come out in a morning thus, with a pleasant face, and to make my friends merry, that all's well within.

But I have cares that would break a heart of stone. My wife has so encroached upon every one of my privileges, that I'm now no more than a mere lodger in my own house.

Hon. But a little spirit exerted on your side might perhaps restore your authority.

Cro. No, though I had the spirit of a lion ! I do rouse sometimes. But what then ? always haggling and haggling. A man is tired of getting the better before his wife is tired of losing the victory.

Hon. It's a melancholy consideration indeed, that our chief comforts often produce our greatest anxieties, and that an increase of our possessions is but an inlet to new disquietudes.

Cro. Ah, my dear friend, these were the very words of poor Dick Doleful to me not a week before he made away with himself. Indeed, Mr. Honeywood, I never see you but you put me in mind of poor Dick. Ah, there was merit neglected for you ! and so true a friend ! we loved each other for thirty years, and yet he never asked me to lend him a single farthing.

Hon. Pray what could induce him to commit so rash an action at last ?

Cro. I don't know : some people were malicious enough to say it was keeping company with me ; because we used to meet now and then and open our hearts to each other. To be sure I loved to hear him talk, and he loved to hear me talk ; poor dear Dick ! He used to say that Croaker rhymed to joker ; and so we used to laugh.—Poor Dick !   [*Going to cry.*

Hon. His fate affects me.

Cro. Ah, he grew sick of this miserable life, where we do nothing but eat and grow hungry, dress and undress, get up and lie down ; while reason, that should watch like a nurse by our side, falls as fast asleep as we do.

Hon. To say a truth, if we compare that part of life which is to come, by that which we have passed, the prospect is hideous.

Cro. Life at the greatest and best is but a froward child, that must be humoured and coaxed a little till it falls asleep, and then all the care is over.

Hon. Very true, sir ; nothing can exceed the vanity of our existence, but the folly of our pursuits. We wept when we came into the world, and every day tells us why.

Cro. Ah, my dear friend, it is a perfect satisfaction to be miserable with you. My son Leontine shan't lose the benefit of such fine conversation. I'll just step home for him. I am willing to show him so much seriousness in one scarce older than himself. And what if I bring my last letter to the *Gazetteer* on the increase and progress of earthquakes ? It will amuse us, I promise you. I there prove how the late earthquake is coming round to pay us another visit, from London to Lisbon, from Lisbon to the Canary Islands, from the Canary Islands to Palmyra, from Palmyra to Constantinople, and so from Constantinople back to London again. [*Exit.*

Hon. Poor Croaker ! his situation deserves the utmost pity. I shall scarce recover my spirits these three days. Sure, to live upon such terms is worse than death itself ! And yet, when I consider my own situation,—a broken fortune, a hopeless passion, friends in distress, the wish but not the power to serve them—(*pausing and sighing.*)

Enter BUTLER.

But. More company below, sir ; Mrs. Croaker and Miss Richland : shall I show them up ? but they're showing up themselves. [*Exit.*

Enter MRS. CROAKER *and* MISS RICHLAND.

Miss Rich. You're always in such spirits.

Mrs. Cro. We have just come, my dear Honeywood, from the auction. There was the old deaf dowager, as usual, bidding like a fury against herself. And then so curious in antiques! herself the most genuine piece of antiquity in the whole collection.

Hon. Excuse me, ladies, if some uneasiness from friendship makes me unfit to share in this good-humour : I know you'll pardon me.

Mrs. Cro. I vow he seems as melancholy as if he had taken a dose of my husband this morning. Well, if Richland here can pardon you, I must.

Miss Rich. You would seem to insinuate, madam, that I have particular reasons for being disposed to refuse it.

Mrs. Cro. Whatever I insinuate, my dear, don't be so ready to wish an explanation.

Miss Rich. I own I should be sorry Mr. Honeywood's long friendship and mine should be misunderstood.

Hon. There's no answering for others, madam. But I hope you'll never find me presuming to offer more than the most delicate friendship may readily allow.

Miss Rich. And I shall be prouder of such a tribute from you, than the most passionate professions from others.

Hon. My own sentiments, madam : friendship is a disinterested commerce between equals ; love, an abject intercourse between tyrants and slaves.

Miss Rich. And, without a compliment, I know none more disinterested, or more capable of friendship, than Mr. Honeywood.

Mrs. Cro. And, indeed, I know nobody that has more friends, at least among the ladies. Miss Fruzz, Miss Oddbody, and Miss Winterbottom, praise him in all companies. As for Miss Biddy Bundle, she's his professed admirer.

Miss Rich. Indeed! an admirer! I did not know, sir, you were such a favourite there. But is she seriously so handsome? Is she the mighty thing talked of?

Hon. The town, madam, seldom begins to praise a lady's beauty, till she's beginning to lose it—(*smiling*).

Mrs. Cro. But she's resolved never to lose it, it seems ;

for, as her natural face decays, her skill improves in making the artificial one. Well, nothing diverts me more than one of these fine, old, dressy things, who thinks to conceal her age, by everywhere exposing her person ; sticking herself up in the front of a side-box ; trailing through a minuet at Almack's ; and then, in the public gardens, looking for all the world like one of the painted ruins of the place.

Hon. Every age has its admirers, ladies. While you, perhaps, are trading among the warmer climates of youth, there ought to be some to carry on a useful commerce in the frozen latitudes beyond fifty.

Miss Rich. But, then, the mortifications they must suffer before they can be fitted out for traffic. I have seen one of them fret a whole morning at her hair-dresser, when all the fault was her face.

Hon. And yet, I'll engage, has carried that face at last to a very good market. This good-natured town, madam, has husbands, like spectacles, to fit every age, from fifteen to fourscore.

Mrs. Cro. Well, you're a dear, good-natured creature. But you know you're engaged with us this morning upon a strolling party. I want to show Olivia the town, and the things ; I believe I shall have business for you for the whole day.

Hon. I am sorry, madam, I have an appointment with Mr. Croaker, which it is impossible to put off.

Mrs. Cro. What ! with my husband ? Then I'm resolved to take no refusal. Nay, I protest you must. You know I never laugh so much as with you.

Hon. Why, if I must, I must. I'll swear you have put me into such spirits. Well, do you find jest, and I'll find laugh, I promise you. We'll wait for the chariot in the next room. [*Exeunt.*

Enter LEONTINE *and* OLIVIA.

Leon. There they go, thoughtless and happy. My dearest Olivia, what would I give to see you capable of sharing in their amusements, and as cheerful as they are !

Oliv. How, my Leontine, how can I be cheerful, when I have so many terrors to oppress me ? The fear of being detected by this family, and the apprehensions of a censuring world, when I must be detected——

Leon. The world, my love ! what can it say ? At worst it can only say that, being compelled by a mercenary guardian to embrace a life you disliked, you formed a resolution of flying with the man of your choice ; that you confided in his honour, and took refuge in my father's house ; the only one where yours could remain without censure.

Oliv. But consider, Leontine, your disobedience and my indiscretion ; your being sent to France to bring home a sister, and, instead of a sister, bringing home——

Leon. One dearer than a thousand sisters. One that I am convinced will be equally dear to the rest of the family, when she comes to be known.

Oliv. And that, I fear, will shortly be.

Leon. Impossible, till we ourselves think proper to make the discovery. My sister, you know, has been with her aunt, at Lyons, since she was a child, and you find every creature in the family takes you for her.

Oliv. But mayn't she write, mayn't her aunt write ?

Leon. Her aunt scarce ever writes, and all my sister's letters are directed to me.

Oliv. But won't your refusing Miss Richland, for whom you know the old gentleman intends you, create a suspicion ?

Leon. There, there's my master-stroke. I have resolved not to refuse her ; nay, an hour hence I have consented to go with my father to make her an offer of my heart and fortune.

Oliv. Your heart and fortune !

Leon. Don't be alarmed, my dearest. Can Olivia think so meanly of my honour or my love, as to suppose I could ever hope for happiness from any but her ? No, my Olivia, neither the force, nor, permit me to add, the delicacy of my passion, leaves any room to suspect me. I only offer Miss Richland a heart I am convinced she will refuse ; as I am confident that, without knowing it, her affections are fixed upon Mr. Honeywood.

Oliv. Mr. Honeywood! You'll excuse my apprehensions ; but when your merits come to be put in the balance——

Leon. You view them with too much partiality. However, by making this offer, I show a seeming compliance with my father's command ; and, perhaps, upon her refusal, I may have his consent to choose for myself.

Oliv. Well, I submit. And yet, my Leontine, I own I shall envy her even your pretended addresses. I consider every look, every expression of your esteem, as due only to me. This is folly, perhaps : I allow it : but it is natural to suppose, that merit which has made an impression on one's own heart, may be powerful over that of another.

Leon. Don't, my life's treasure, don't let us make imaginary evils, when you know we have so many real ones to encounter. At worst, you know, if Miss Richland should consent, or my father refuse his pardon, it can but end in a trip to Scotland ; and——

Enter CROAKER.

Cro. Where have you been, boy ? I have been seeking you. My friend Honeywood here has been saying such comfortable things. Ah ! he's an example indeed. Where is he ? I left him here.

Leon. Sir, I believe you may see him, and hear him too, in the next room ; he's preparing to go out with the ladies.

Cro. Good gracious ! can I believe my eyes or my ears ! I'm struck dumb with his vivacity, and stunned with the loudness of his laugh. Was there ever such a transformation ! (*A laugh behind the scenes.* CROAKER *mimics it.*) Ha! ha! ha! there it goes: a plague take their balderdash! Yet I could expect nothing less, when my precious wife was of the party. On my conscience, I believe she could spread a horse-laugh through the pews of a tabernacle.

Leon. Since you find so many objections to a wife, sir, how can you be so earnest in recommending one to me?

Cro. I have told you, and tell you again, boy, that Miss Richland's fortune must not go out of the family; one may find comfort in the money, whatever one does in the wife.

Leon. But, sir, though, in obedience to your desire, I am ready to marry her, it may be possible she has no inclination to me.

Cro. I'll tell you once for all how it stands. A good part of Miss Richland's large fortune consists in a claim upon Government, which my good friend, Mr. Lofty, assures me the Treasury will allow. One half of this she is to forfeit, by her father's will, in case she refuses to marry you. So, if she rejects you, we seize half her fortune; if she accepts you, we seize the whole, and a fine girl into the bargain.

Leon. But, sir, if you will but listen to reason——

Cro. Come, then, produce your reasons. I tell you, I'm fixed, determined; so now produce your reasons. When I'm determined, I always listen to reason, because it can then do no harm.

Leon. You have alleged that a mutual choice was the first requisite in matrimonial happiness.

Cro. Well, and you have both of you a mutual choice. She has her choice—to marry you, or lose half her fortune; and you have your choice—to marry her, or pack out of doors without any fortune at all.

Leon. An only son, sir, might expect more indulgence.

Cro. An only father, sir, might expect more obedience: besides, has not your sister here, that never disobliged me in her life, as good a right as you? He's a sad dog, Livy, my dear, and would take all from you. But he shan't, I tell you he shan't, for you shall have your share.

Oliv. Dear sir, I wish you'd be convinced, that I can never be happy in any addition to my fortune which is taken from his.

Cro. Well, well, it's a good child, so say no more : but come with me, and we shall see something that will give us a great deal of pleasure, I promise you ; old Ruggins, the curry-comb maker, lying in state : I am told he makes a very handsome corpse, and becomes his coffin prodigiously. He was an intimate friend of mine, and these are friendly things we ought to do for each other.

[*Exeunt.*

ACT THE SECOND

SCENE—CROAKER'S *House*.

MISS RICHLAND *and* GARNET.

Miss Rich. Olivia not his sister ?   Olivia not Leontine's sister ?   You amaze me !

Gar. No more his sister than I am ; I had it all from
his own servant : I can get anything from that quarter.

Miss Rich. But how ?   Tell me again, Garnet.

Gar. Why, madam, as I told you before, instead of
going to Lyons to bring home his sister, who has been
there with her aunt these ten years, he never went farther
than Paris : there he saw and fell in love with this young
lady—by the bye, of a prodigious family.

Miss Rich. And brought her home to my guardian
as his daughter ?

Gar. Yes, and daughter she will be.   If he don't
consent to their marriage, they talk of trying what a
Scotch parson can do.

Miss Rich. Well, I own they have deceived me—And
so demurely as Olivia carried it too !—Would you believe
it, Garnet, I told her all my secrets ; and yet the sly
cheat concealed all this from me ?

Gar. And, upon my word, madam, I don't much blame
her : she was loth to trust one with her secrets, that was
so very bad at keeping her own.

Miss Rich. But, to add to their deceit, the young
gentleman, it seems, pretends to make me serious proposals.   My guardian and he are to be here presently, to

open the affair in form. You know I am to lose half my fortune if I refuse him.

Gar. Yet, what can you do ? For being, as you are, in love with Mr. Honeywood, madam——

Miss Rich. How ! idiot, what do you mean ? In love with Mr. Honeywood ! Is this to provoke me ?

Gar. That is, madam, in friendship with him ; I meant nothing more than friendship, as I hope to be married ; nothing more.

Miss Rich. Well, no more of this. As to my guardian and his son, they shall find me prepared to receive them : I'm resolved to accept their proposal with seeming pleasure, to mortify them by compliance, and so throw the refusal at last upon them.

Gar. Delicious ! and that will secure your whole fortune to yourself. Well, who could have thought so innocent a face could cover so much 'cuteness !

Miss Rich. Why, girl, I only oppose my prudence to their cunning, and practise a lesson they have taught me against themselves.

Gar. Then you're likely not long to want employment, for here they come, and in close conference.

Enter CROAKER *and* LEONTINE.

Leon. Excuse me, sir, if I seem to hesitate upon the point of putting to the lady so important a question.

Cro. Lord ! good sir, moderate your fears ; you're so plaguy shy, that one would think you had changed sexes. I tell you we must have the half or the whole. Come, let me see with what spirit you begin. Well, why don't you ? Eh ! what ? Well, then—I must, it seems— Miss Richland, my dear, I believe you guess at our business ; an affair which my son here comes to open, that nearly concerns your happiness.

Miss Rich. Sir, I should be ungrateful not to be pleased with anything that comes recommended by you.

Cro. How, boy, could you desire a finer opening ? Why don't you begin, I say ? [*To* LEONTINE.

Leon. 'Tis true, madam, my father, madam, has some intentions—hem—of explaining an affair—which—himself—can best explain, madam.

Cro. Yes, my dear ; it comes entirely from my son ; it's all a request of his own, madam. And I will permit him to make the best of it.

Leon. The whole affair is only this, madam ; my father has a proposal to make, which he insists none but himself shall deliver.

Cro. My mind misgives me, the fellow will never be brought on (*aside*.) In short, madam, you see before you one that loves you, one whose whole happiness is all in you.

Miss Rich. I never had any doubts of your regard, sir ; and I hope you can have none of my duty.

Cro. That's not the thing, my little sweeting ; my love ! No, no, another-guess lover than I : there he stands, madam, his very looks declare the force of his passion—Call up a look, you dog ! (*aside*)—But then, had you seen him, as I have, weeping, speaking soliloquies and blank verse, sometimes melancholy, and sometimes absent.

Miss Rich. I fear, sir, he's absent now ; or such a declaration would have come most properly from himself.

Cro. Himself, madam ! he would die before he could make such a confession ; and if he had not a channel for his passion through me, it would ere now have drowned his understanding.

Miss Rich. I must grant, sir, there are attractions in modest diffidence above the force of words. A silent address is the genuine eloquence of sincerity.

Cro. Madam, he has forgot to speak any other language ; silence is become his mother-tongue.

Miss Rich. And it must be confessed, sir, it speaks very powerfully in his favour. And yet I shall be thought too forward in making such a confession ; shan't I, Mr. Leontine ?

Leon. Confusion! my reserve will undo me. But, if modesty attracts her, impudence may disgust her. I'll try (*aside*). Don't imagine from my silence, madam, that I want a due sense of the honour and happiness intended me. My father, madam, tells me, your humble servant is not totally indifferent to you—he admires you: I adore you; and when we come together, upon my soul I believe we shall be the happiest couple in all St. James's.

Miss Rich. If I could flatter myself you thought as you speak, sir——

Leon. Doubt my sincerity, madam? By your dear self I swear. Ask the brave if they desire glory? ask cowards if they covet safety——

Cro. Well, well, no more questions about it.

Leon. Ask the sick if they long for health? ask misers if they love money? ask——

Cro. Ask a fool if he can talk nonsense! What's come over the boy? What signifies asking, when there's not a soul to give you an answer? If you would ask to the purpose, ask this lady's consent to make you happy.

Miss Rich. Why indeed, sir, his uncommon ardour almost compels me—forces me to comply. And yet I'm afraid he'll despise a conquest gained with too much ease; won't you, Mr. Leontine?

Leon. Confusion! (*aside.*) Oh, by no means, madam, by no means. And yet, madam, you talked of force. There is nothing I would avoid so much as compulsion in a thing of this kind. No, madam, I will still be generous, and leave you at liberty to refuse.

Cro. But I tell you, sir, the lady is not at liberty. It's a match. You see she says nothing. Silence gives consent.

Leon. But, sir, she talked of force. Consider, sir, the cruelty of constraining her inclinations.

Cro. But I say there's no cruelty. Don't you know, blockhead, that girls have always a roundabout way of saying yes before company? So get you both gone

together into the next room, and hang him that inter-
rupts the tender explanation. Get you gone, I say; I'll
not hear a word.

Leon. But, sir, I must beg leave to insist——

Cro. Get off, you puppy, or I'll beg leave to insist upon
knocking you down. Stupid whelp! But I don't
wonder: the boy takes entirely after his mother.

[*Exeunt* MISS RICHLAND *and* LEONTINE.

Enter MRS. CROAKER.

Mrs. Cro. Mr. Croaker, I bring you something, my
dear, that I believe will make you smile.

Cro. I'll hold you a guinea of that, my dear.

Mrs. Cro. A letter; and, as I knew the hand, I
ventured to open it.

Cro. And how can you expect your breaking open my
letters should give me pleasure?

Mrs. Cro. Poo! it's from your sister at Lyons, and
contains good news; read it.

Cro. What a Frenchified cover is here! That sister
of mine has some good qualities, but I could never teach
her to fold a letter.

Mrs. Cro. Fold a fiddlestick! Read what it contains.

CROAKER, *reading.*

"DEAR NICK,—An English gentleman, of large fortune,
has for some time made private, though honourable
proposals to your daughter Olivia. They love each
other tenderly, and I find she has consented, without
letting any of the family know, to crown his addresses.
As such good offers don't come every day, your own
good sense, his large fortune, and family considerations,
will induce you to forgive her.—Yours ever,
"RACHAEL CROAKER."

My daughter Olivia privately contracted to a man of
large fortune! This is good news, indeed. My heart never
foretold me of this. And yet, how slily the little bag-

gage has carried it since she came home ; not a word on't to the old ones for the world. Yet I thought I saw something she wanted to conceal.

Mrs. Cro. Well, if they have concealed their amour, they shan't conceal their wedding ; that shall be public, I'm resolved.

Cro. I tell thee, woman, the wedding is the most foolish part of the ceremony. I can never get this woman to think of the most serious part of the nuptial engagement.

Mrs. Cro. What would you have me think of, their funeral ? But come, tell me, my dear, don't you owe more to me than you care to confess ? Would you have ever been known to Mr. Lofty, who has undertaken Miss Richland's claim at the Treasury, but for me ? Who was it first made him an acquaintance at Lady Shabbaroon's rout ? Who got him to promise us his interest ? Is not he a backstairs favourite, one that can do what he pleases with those that do what they please ? Is not he an acquaintance that all your groaning and lamentation could never have got us ?

Cro. He is a man of importance, I grant you. And yet what amazes me is, that, while he is giving away places to all the world, he can't get one for himself.

Mrs. Cro. That perhaps may be owing to his nicety. Great men are not easily satisfied.

Enter French Servant.

Ser. An expresse from Monsieur Lofty. He vil be vait upon your honours instammant. He be only giving four five instruction, read two tree memorial, call upon von ambassadeur. He vil be vid you in one tree minutes.

Mrs. Cro. You see now, my dear. What an extensive department ! Well, friend, let your master know, that we are extremely honoured by this honour. Was there anything ever in a higher style of breeding ? All mes-sages among the great are now done by express.

Cro. To be sure, no man does little things with more solemnity, or claims more respect than he. But he's in the right on't. In our bad world, respect is given where respect is claimed.

Mrs. Cro. Never mind the world, my dear; you were never in a pleasanter place in your life. Let us now think of receiving him with proper respect—(*A loud rapping at the door*),—and there he is, by the thundering rap.

Cro. Ay, verily, there he is! as close upon the heels of his own express, as an endorsement upon the back of a bill. Well, I'll leave you to receive him, whilst I go to chide my little Olivia for intending to steal a marriage without mine or her aunt's consent. I must seem to be angry, or she too may begin to despise my authority.

[*Exit.*

Enter LOFTY, *speaking to his* Servant.

Lof. " And if the Venetian ambassador, or that teasing creature the Marquis, should call, I'm not at home. Dam'me, I'll be pack-horse to none of them." My dear madam, I have just snatched a moment— " And if the expresses to his grace be ready, let them be sent off; they're of importance."—Madam, I ask a thousand pardons.

Mrs. Cro. Sir, this honour——

Lof. " And, Dubardieu! if the person calls about the commission, let him know that it is made out. As for Lord Cumbercourt's stale request, it can keep cold: you understand me."—Madam, I ask ten thousand pardons.

Mrs. Cro. Sir, this honour——

Lof. " And, Dubardieu! if the man comes from the Cornish borough, you must do him; you must do him, I say."—Madam, I ask ten thousand pardons.—" And if the Russian ambassador calls; but he will scarce call to-day, I believe."—And now, madam, I have just got time to express my happiness in having the honour of being permitted to profess myself your most obedient, humble servant.

Mrs. Cro. Sir, the happiness and honour are all mine ; and yet, I'm only robbing the public while I detain you.

Lof. Sink the public, madam, when the fair are to be attended. Ah, could all my hours be so charmingly devoted ! Sincerely, don't you pity us poor creatures in affairs ? Thus it is eternally ; solicited for places here, teased for pensions there, and courted everywhere. I know you pity me. Yes, I see you do.

Mrs. Cro. Excuse me, sir, " Toils of empires pleasures are," as Waller says.

Lof. Waller, Waller, is he of the house ?

Mrs. Cro. The modern poet of that name, sir.

Lof. Oh, a modern ! We men of business despise the moderns ; and as for the ancients, we have no time to read them. Poetry is a pretty thing enough for our wives and daughters ; but not for us. Why now, here I stand that know nothing of books. I say, madam, I know nothing of books ; and yet, I believe, upon a land-carriage fishery, a stamp act, or a jag-hire, I can talk my two hours without feeling the want of them.

Mrs. Cro. The world is no stranger to Mr. Lofty's eminence in every capacity.

Lof. I vow to gad, madam, you make me blush. I'm nothing, nothing, nothing in the world ; a mere obscure gentleman. To be sure, indeed, one or two of the present ministers are pleased to represent me as a formidable man. I know they are pleased to bespatter me at all their little dirty levees. Yet, upon my soul, I wonder what they see in me to treat me so ! Measures, not men, have always been my mark ; and I vow, by all that's honourable, my resentment has never done the men, as mere men, any manner of harm—that is, as mere men.

Mrs. Cro. What importance, and yet what modesty !

Lof. Oh, if you talk of modesty, madam, there, I own, I'm accessible to praise : modesty is my foible : it was so the Duke of Brentford used to say of me. "I love Jack Lofty," he used to say: "no man has a finer knowledge of things; quite a man of information; and when he speaks upon his legs, by the Lord he's prodigious, he scouts them; and yet all men have their faults; too much modesty is his," says his grace.

Mrs. Cro. And yet, I dare say, you don't want assurance when you come to solicit for your friends.

Lof. Oh, there indeed I'm in bronze. Apropos! I have just been mentioning Miss Richland's case to a certain personage; we must name no names. When I ask, I am not to be put off, madam. No, no, I take my friend by the button. A fine girl, sir; great justice in her case. A friend of mine—borough interest—business must be done, Mr. Secretary.—I say, Mr. Secretary, her business must be done, sir. That's my way, madam.

Mrs. Cro. Bless me! you said all this to the Secretary of State, did you?

Lof. I did not say the Secretary, did I? Well, curse it, since you have found me out, I will not deny it. It was to the Secretary.

Mrs. Cro. This was going to the fountain-head at once, not applying to the understrappers, as Mr. Honeywood would have had us.

Lof. Honeywood! he! he! he! He was, indeed, a fine solicitor. I suppose you have heard what has just happened to him?

Mrs. Cro. Poor dear man! no accident, I hope?

Lof. Undone, madam, that's all. His creditors have taken him into custody. A prisoner in his own house.

Mrs. Cro. A prisoner in his own house? How! At this very time? I'm quite unhappy for him.

Lof. Why, so am I. The man, to be sure, was immensely good-natured. But then I could never find that he had anything in him.

Mrs. Cro. His manner, to be sure, was excessively

harmless; some, indeed, thought it a little dull. For my part, I always concealed my opinion.

Lof. It can't be concealed, madam; the man was dull, dull as the last new comedy! a poor impracticable creature! I tried once or twice to know if he was fit for business; but he had scarce talents to be groom-porter to an orange-barrow.

Mrs. Cro. How differently does Miss Richland think of him! for, I believe, with all his faults, she loves him.

Lof. Loves him! Does she? You should cure her of that by all means. Let me see; what if she were sent to him this instant, in his present doleful situation? My life for it, that works her cure. Distress is a perfect antidote to love. Suppose we join her in the next room? Miss Richland is a fine girl, has a fine fortune, and must not be thrown away. Upon my honour, madam, I have a regard for Miss Richland; and rather than she should be thrown away, I should think it no indignity to marry her myself. [*Exeunt.*

Enter OLIVIA *and* LEONTINE.

Leon. And yet, trust me, Olivia, I had every reason to expect Miss Richland's refusal, as I did everything in my power to deserve it. Her indelicacy surprises me.

Oliv. Sure, Leontine, there's nothing so indelicate in being sensible of your merit. If so, I fear I shall be the most guilty thing alive.

Leon. But you mistake, my dear. The same attention I used to advance my merit with you, I practised to lessen it with her. What more could I do?

Oliv. Let us now rather consider what is to be done. We have both dissembled too long.—I have always been ashamed—I am now quite weary of it. Sure I could never have undergone so much for any other but you.

Leon. And you shall find my gratitude equal to your

7 *a*

kindest compliance. Though our friends should totally forsake us, Olivia, we can draw upon content for the deficiencies of fortune.

Oliv. Then why should we defer our scheme of humble happiness, when it is now in our power ? I may be the favourite of your father, it is true ; but can it ever be thought, that his present kindness to a supposed child will continue to a known deceiver ?

Leon. I have many reasons to believe it will. As his attachments are but few, they are lasting. His own marriage was a private one, as ours may be. Besides, I have sounded him already at a distance, and find all his answers exactly to our wish. Nay, by an expression or two that dropped from him, I am induced to think he knows of this affair.

Oliv. Indeed ! But that would be a happiness too great to be expected.

Leon. However it be, I'm certain you have power over him ; and I am persuaded, if you informed him of our situation, that he would be disposed to pardon it.

Oliv. You had equal expectations, Leontine, from your last scheme with Miss Richland, which you find has succeeded most wretchedly.

Leon. And that's the best reason for trying another.

Oliv. If it must be so, I submit.

Leon. As we could wish, he comes this way. Now, my dearest Olivia, be resolute. I'll just retire within hearing, to come in at a proper time, either to share your danger, or confirm your victory. [*Exit.*

Enter CROAKER.

Cro. Yes, I must forgive her ; and yet not too easily, neither. It will be proper to keep up the decorums of resentment a little, if it be only to impress her with an idea of my authority.

Oliv. How I tremble to approach him !—Might I presume, sir,—if I interrupt you——

Cro. No, child, where I have an affection, it is not a little thing that can interrupt me. Affection gets over little things.

Oliv. Sir, you're too kind. I'm sensible how ill I deserve this partiality. Yet, Heaven knows, there is nothing I would not do to gain it.

Cro. And you have but too well succeeded, you little hussy, you! With those endearing ways of yours, on my conscience, I could be brought to forgive anything, unless it were a very great offence indeed.

Oliv. But mine is such an offence—When you know my guilt—Yes, you shall know it, though I feel the greatest pain in the confession.

Cro. Why, then, if it be so very great a pain, you may spare yourself the trouble; for I know every syllable of the matter before you begin.

Oliv. Indeed! then I'm undone.

Cro. Ay, miss, you wanted to steal a match, without letting me know it, did you? But I'm not worth being consulted, I suppose, when there's to be a marriage in my own family. No, I'm nobody. I'm to be a mere article of family lumber; a piece of cracked china to be stuck up in a corner.

Oliv. Dear sir, nothing but the dread of your authority could induce us to conceal it from you.

Cro. No, no, my consequence is no more; I'm as little minded as a dead Russian in winter, just stuck up with a pipe in its mouth till there comes a thaw—It goes to my heart to vex her (*aside*).

Oliv. I was prepared, sir, for your anger, and despaired of pardon, even while I presumed to ask it. But your severity shall never abate my affection, as my punishment is but justice.

Cro. And yet you should not despair neither, Livy. We ought to hope all for the best.

Oliv. And do you permit me to hope, sir? Can I ever expect to be forgiven? But hope has too long deceived me.

Cro. Why then, child, it shan't deceive you now, for I forgive you this very moment ; I forgive you all ; and now you are indeed my daughter.

Oliv. O transport ! this kindness overpowers me.

Cro. I was always against severity to our children. We have been young and giddy ourselves, and we can't expect boys and girls to be old before their time.

Oliv. What generosity ! but can you forget the many falsehoods, the dissimulation——

Cro. You did indeed dissemble, you urchin, you ; but where's the girl that won't dissemble for a husband ? My wife and I had never been married, if we had not dissembled a little beforehand.

Oliv. It shall be my future care never to put such generosity to a second trial. And as for the partner of my offence and folly, from his native honour, and the just sense he has of his duty, I can answer for him that——

Enter LEONTINE.

Leon. Permit him thus to answer for himself (*kneeling*). Thus, sir, let me speak my gratitude for this unmerited forgiveness. Yes, sir, this even exceeds all your former tenderness. I now can boast the most indulgent of fathers. The life he gave, compared to this, was but a trifling blessing.

Cro. And, good sir, who sent for you, with that fine tragedy face, and flourishing manner ? I don't know what we have to do with your gratitude upon this occasion.

Leon. How, sir ! Is it possible to be silent, when so much obliged ? Would you refuse me the pleasure of being grateful ? of adding my thanks to my Olivia's ? of sharing in the transports that you have thus occasioned ?

Cro. Lord, sir, we can be happy enough without your coming in to make up the party. I don't know what's the matter with the boy all this day ; he has got into such a rhodomontade manner all this morning !

Leon. But, sir, I that have so large a part in the benefit, is it not my duty to show my joy ? is the being admitted to your favour so slight an obligation ? is the happiness of marrying my Olivia so small a blessing ?

Cro. Marrying Olivia ! marrying Olivia ! marrying his own sister ! Sure the boy is out of his senses ! His own sister !

Leon. My sister !

Oliv. Sister ! How have I been mistaken ! (*Aside.*)

Leon. Some cursed mistake in all this, I find ! (*Aside.*)

Cro. What does the booby mean ? or has he any meaning ? Eh, what do you mean, you blockhead, you ?

Leon. Mean, sir—why, sir—only, when my sister is to be married, that I have the pleasure of marrying her, sir ; that is, of giving her away, sir—I have made a point of it.

Cro. Oh, is that all ? Give her away. You have made a point of it. Then you had as good make a point of first giving away yourself, as I'm going to prepare the writings between you and Miss Richland this very minute. What a fuss is here about nothing ! Why, what's the matter now ? I thought I had made you at least as happy as you could wish.

Oliv. Oh yes, sir ; very happy.

Cro. Do you foresee anything, child ? You look as if you did. I think if anything was to be foreseen, I have as sharp a look-out as another ; and yet I foresee nothing.

[*Exit.*

Oliv. What can it mean ?

Leon. He knows something, and yet for my life I can't tell what.

Oliv. It can't be the connection between us, I'm pretty certain.

Leon. Whatever it be, my dearest, I am resolved to put it out of fortune's power to repeat our mortification.

I'll haste and prepare for our journey to Scotland this very evening. My friend Honeywood has promised me his advice and assistance. I'll go to him, and repose our distresses on his friendly bosom ; and I know so much of his honest heart, that if he can't relieve our uneasiness, he will at least share them. [*Exeunt.*

ACT THE THIRD

Scene—*Young* HONEYWOOD'S *House.*

BAILIFF, HONEYWOOD, Follower.

Bail. Lookye, sir, I have arrested as good men as you in my time : no disparagement of you neither : men that would go forty guineas on a game of cribbage. I challenge the town to show a man in more genteeler practice than myself.

Hon. Without all question, Mr. ——. I forget your name, sir.

Bail. How can you forget what you never knew ? he ! he ! he !

Hon. May I beg leave to ask your name ?

Bail. Yes, you may.

Hon. Then, pray, sir, what is your name ?

Bail. That I didn't promise to tell you. He ! he ! he ! A joke breaks no bones, as we say among us that practise the law.

Hon. You may have reason for keeping it a secret, perhaps ?

Bail. The law does nothing without reason. I'm ashamed to tell my name to no man, sir. If you can show cause, as why, upon a special capus, that I should prove my name—But, come, Timothy Twitch is my name. And, now you know my name, what have you to say to that ?

Hon. Nothing in the world, good Mr. Twitch, but that I have a favour to ask, that's all.

Bail. Ay, favours are more easily asked than granted, as we say among us that practise the law. I have taken an oath against granting favours. Would you have me perjure myself ?

Hon. But my request will come recommended in so strong a manner, as, I believe, you'll have no scruple (*pulling out his purse*). The thing is only this. I believe I shall be able to discharge this trifle in two or three days at farthest ; but as I would not have the affair known for the world, I have thoughts of keeping you, and your good friend here, about me till the debt is discharged ; for which I shall be properly grateful.

Bail. Oh ! that's another maxum, and altogether within my oath. For certain, if an honest man is to get anything by a thing, there's no reason why all things should not be done in civility.

Hon. Doubtless, all trades must live, Mr. Twitch ; and yours is a necessary one. (*Gives him money.*)

Bail. Oh ! your honour ; I hope your honour takes nothing amiss as I does, as I does nothing but my duty in so doing. I'm sure no man can say I ever give a gentleman, that was a gentleman, ill usage. If I saw that a gentleman was a gentleman, I have taken money not to see him for ten weeks together.

Hon. Tenderness is a virtue, Mr. Twitch.

Bail. Ay, sir, it's a perfect treasure. I love to see a gentleman with a tender heart. I don't know, but I think I have a tender heart myself. If all that I have lost by my heart was put together, it would make a— but no matter for that.

Hon. Don't account it lost, Mr. Twitch. The ingratitude of the world can never deprive us of the conscious happiness of having acted with humanity ourselves.

Bail. Humanity, sir, is a jewel. It's better than gold. I love humanity. People may say, that we in our way have no humanity ; but I'll show you my humanity this moment. There's my follower here, little Flanigan, with a wife and four children ; a guinea or two would be more to him than twice as much to another. Now, as I can't show him any humanity myself, I must beg leave you'll do it for me.

Hon. I assure you, Mr. Twitch, yours is a most powerful recommendation. (*Giving money to the* Follower.)

Bail. Sir, you're a gentleman. I see you know what to do with your money. But to business : we are to be with you here as your friends, I suppose. But set in case company comes. Little Flanigan here, to be sure, has a good face ; a very good face ; but then, he is a little seedy, as we say among us that practise the law. Not well in clothes. Smoke the pocket-holes.

Hon. Well, that shall be remedied without delay.

Enter Servant.

Ser. Sir, Miss Richland is below.

Hon. How unlucky ! Detain her a moment. We must improve my good friend little Mr. Flanigan's appearance first. Here, let Mr. Flanigan have a suit of my clothes—quick—the brown and silver—Do you hear ?

Ser. That your honour gave away to the begging gentleman that makes verses, because it was as good as new.

Hon. The white and gold then.

Ser. That, your honour, I made bold to sell, because it was good for nothing.

Hon. Well, the first that comes to hand then. The blue and gold then. I believe Mr. Flanigan will look best in blue. [*Exit* FLANIGAN.

Bail. Rabbit me, but little Flanigan will look well in anything. Ah, if your honour knew that bit of flesh as well as I do, you'd be perfectly in love with him. There's not a prettier scout in the four counties after a shy-cock than he : scents like a hound ; sticks like a weasel. He was master of the ceremonies to the black Queen of

Morocco, when I took him to follow me. (*Re-enter* FLANIGAN.) Heh, ecod, I think he looks so well, that I don't care if I have a suit from the same place myself.

Hon. Well, well, I hear the lady coming. Dear Mr. Twitch, I beg you'll give your friend directions not to speak. As for yourself, I know you will say nothing without being directed.

Bail. Never you fear me : I'll show the lady that I have something to say for myself as well as another. One man has one way of talking, and another man has another, that's all the difference between them.

Enter MISS RICHLAND *and her* Maid.

Miss Rich. You'll be surprised, sir, with this visit. But you know I've yet to thank you for choosing my little library.

Hon. Thanks, madam, are unnecessary ; as it was I that was obliged by your commands. Chairs here. Two of my very good friends, Mr. Twitch and Mr. Flanigan. Pray, gentlemen, sit without ceremony.

Miss Rich. Who can these odd-looking men be ! I fear it is as I was informed. It must be so. (*Aside.*)

Bail. (*After a pause.*) Pretty weather ; very pretty weather for the time of year, madam.

Fol. Very good circuit weather in the country.

Hon. You officers are generally favourites among the ladies. My friends, madam, have been upon very disagreeable duty, I assure you. The fair should, in some measure, recompense the toils of the brave.

Miss Rich. Our officers do indeed deserve every favour. The gentlemen are in the marine service, I presume, sir.

Hon. Why, madam, they do—occasionally serve in the fleet, madam. A dangerous service !

Miss Rich. I'm told so. And I own it has often surprised me, that while we have had so many instances of bravery there, we have had so few of wit at home to praise it.

Hon. I grant, madam, that our poets have not written as our soldiers have fought ; but they have done all they could, and Hawke or Amherst could do no more.

Miss Rich. I'm quite displeased when I see a fine subject spoiled by a dull writer.

Hon. We should not be so severe against dull writers, madam. It is ten to one but the dullest writer exceeds the most rigid French critic who presumes to despise him.

Fol. Damn the French, the parle vous, and all that belongs to them.

Miss Rich. Sir !

Hon. Ha, ha, ha ! honest Mr. Flanigan. A true English officer, madam ; he's not contented with beating the French, but he will scold them too.

Miss Rich. Yet, Mr. Honeywood, this does not convince me but that severity in criticism is necessary. It was our first adopting the severity of French taste, that has brought them in turn to taste us.

Bail. Taste us ! By the Lord, madam, they devour us. Give monseers but a taste, and I'll be damned but they come in for a bellyful.

Miss Rich. Very extraordinary this !

Fol. But very true. What makes the bread rising ? the parle vous that devour us. What makes the mutton fivepence a pound ? the parle vous that eat it up. What makes the beer threepence-halfpenny a pot ?——

Hon. Ah ! the vulgar rogues ; all will be out (*aside*). Right, gentlemen, very right, upon my word, and quite to the purpose. They draw a parallel, madam, between the mental taste and that of our senses. We are injured as much by the French severity in the one, as by French rapacity in the other. That's their meaning.

Miss Rich. Though I don't see the force of the parallel, yet I'll own, that we should sometimes pardon books, as we do our friends, that have now and then agreeable absurdities to recommend them.

Bail. That's all my eye. The king only can pardon, as the law says : for, set in case——

Hon. I'm quite of your opinion, sir. I see the whole drift of your argument. Yes, certainly, our presuming to pardon any work is arrogating a power that belongs to another. If all have power to condemn, what writer can be free ?

Bail. By his habus corpus. His habus corpus can set him free at any time : for, set in case——

Hon. I'm obliged to you, sir, for the hint. If, madam, as my friend observes, our laws are so careful of a gentle-man's person, sure we ought to be equally careful of his dearer part, his fame.

Fol. Ay, but if so be a man's nabbed, you know——

Hon. Mr. Flanigan, if you spoke for ever, you could not improve the last observation. For my own part, I think it conclusive.

Bail. As for the matter of that, mayhap——

Hon. Nay, sir, give me leave in this instance to be positive. For where is the necessity of censuring works without genius, which must shortly sink of themselves ? what is it, but aiming an unnecessary blow against a victim already under the hands of justice ?

Bail. Justice ! Oh, by the elevens, if you talk about justice, I think I am at home there : for, in a course of law——

Hon. My dear Mr. Twitch, I discern what you'd be at, perfectly ; and I believe the lady must be sensible of the art with which it is introduced. I suppose you perceive the meaning, madam, of his course of law.

Miss Rich. I protest, sir, I do not. I perceive only that you answer one gentleman before he has finished, and the other before he has well begun.

Bail. Madam, you are a gentlewoman, and I will make the matter out. This here question is about severity, and justice, and pardon, and the like of they. Now, to explain the thing——

Hon. Oh ! curse your explanations. (*Aside.*)

Enter Servant.

Ser. Mr. Leontine, sir, below, desires to speak with you upon earnest business.

Hon. That's lucky (*aside*). Dear madam, you'll excuse me and my good friends here, for a few minutes. There are books, madam, to amuse you. Come, gentlemen, you know I make no ceremony with such friends. After you, sir. Excuse me. Well, if I must. But I know your natural politeness.

Bail. Before and behind, you know.

Fol. Ay, ay, before and behind, before and behind.

[*Exeunt* HONEYWOOD, BAILIFF, *and* Follower.

Miss Rich. What can all this mean, Garnet?

Gar. Mean, madam! why, what should it mean, but what Mr. Lofty sent you here to see? These people he calls officers are officers sure enough; sheriff's officers; bailiffs, madam.

Miss Rich. Ay, it is certainly so. Well, though his perplexities are far from giving me pleasure, yet I own there is something very ridiculous in them, and a just punishment for his dissimulation.

Gar. And so they are. But I wonder, madam, that the lawyer you just employed to pay his debts, and set him free, has not done it by this time. He ought at least to have been here before now. But lawyers are always more ready to get a man into troubles than out of them.

Enter SIR WILLIAM HONEYWOOD.

Sir Wil. For Miss Richland to undertake setting him free, I own, was quite unexpected. It has totally unhinged my schemes to reclaim him. Yet it gives me pleasure to find that, among a number of worthless friendships, he has made one acquisition of real value; for there must be some softer passion on her side that prompts this generosity. Ha! here before me: I'll endeavour to sound her affections.——Madam, as I am the person that have had some demands upon the gentleman of this house, I hope you'll excuse me, if before I enlarged him, I wanted to see yourself.

Miss Rich. The precaution was very unnecessary, sir. I suppose your wants were only such as my agent had power to satisfy.

Sir Wil. Partly, madam. But I was also willing you should be fully apprised of the character of the gentleman you intended to serve.

Miss Rich. It must come, sir, with a very ill grace from you. To censure it after what you have done, would look like malice ; and to speak favourably of a character you have oppressed, would be impeaching your own. And sure, his tenderness, his humanity, his universal friendship, may atone for many faults.

Sir Wil. That friendship, madam, which is exerted in too wide a sphere, becomes totally useless. Our bounty, like a drop of water, disappears when diffused too widely. They who pretend most to this universal benevolence are either deceivers or dupes : men who desire to cover their private ill-nature by a pretended regard for all ; or men who, reasoning themselves into false feelings, are more earnest in pursuit of splendid, than of useful virtues.

Miss Rich. I am surprised, sir, to hear one, who has probably been a gainer by the folly of others, so severe in his censure of it.

Sir Wil. Whatever I may have gained by folly, madam, you see I am willing to prevent your losing by it.

Miss Rich. Your cares for me, sir, are unnecessary. I always suspect those services which are denied where they are wanted, and offered, perhaps, in hopes of a refusal. No, sir, my directions have been given, and I insist upon their being complied with.

Sir Wil. Thou amiable woman ! I can no longer contain the expressions of my gratitude, my pleasure. You see before you one who has been equally careful of his interest ; one, who has for some time been a concealed spectator of his follies, and only punished in hopes to reclaim him—his uncle !

Miss Rich. Sir William Honeywood ! You amaze me. How shall I conceal my confusion ? I fear, sir, you'll think I have been too forward in my services. I confess I——

Sir Wil. Don't make any apologies, madam. I only find myself unable to repay the obligation. And yet, I have been trying my interest of late to serve you. Having learnt, madam, that you had some demands upon Government, I have, though unasked, been your solicitor there.

Miss Rich. Sir, I'm infinitely obliged to your intentions. But my guardian has employed another gentleman, who assures him of success.

Sir Wil. Who ? The important little man that visits here ? Trust me, madam, he's quite contemptible among men in power, and utterly unable to serve you. Mr. Lofty's promises are much better known to people of fashion, than his person, I assure you.

Miss Rich. How have we been deceived ! As sure as can be, here he comes.

Sir. Wil. Does he ? Remember I'm to continue unknown. My return to England has not yet been made public. With what impudence he enters !

Enter LOFTY.

Lof. Let the chariot—let my chariot drive off ; I'll visit to his grace's in a chair. Miss Richland here before me ! Punctual, as usual, to the calls of humanity. I'm very sorry, madam, things of this kind should happen, especially to a man I have shown everywhere, and carried amongst us as a particular acquaintance.

Miss Rich. I find, sir, you have the art of making the misfortunes of others your own.

Lof. My dear madam, what can a private man like me do ? One man can't do everything ; and then, I do so much in this way every day. Let me see ; something considerable might be done for him by subscription ; it could not fail if I carried the list. I'll undertake to set down a brace of dukes, two dozen lords, and half the lower house, at my own peril.

Sir Wil. And, after all, it's more than probable, sir, he might reject the offer of such powerful patronage.

Lof. Then, madam, what can we do ? You know I never make promises. In truth, I once or twice tried to do something with him in the way of business ; but, as I often told his uncle, Sir William Honeywood, the man was utterly impracticable.

Sir. Wil. His uncle ! then that gentleman, I suppose, is a particular friend of yours.

Lof. Meaning me, sir ?—Yes, madam, as I often said, my dear Sir William, you are sensible I would do anything, as far as my poor interest goes, to serve your family : but what can be done ? there's no procuring first-rate places for ninth-rate abilities.

Miss Rich. I have heard of Sir William Honeywood ; he's abroad in employment : he confided in your judgment, I suppose.

Lof. Why, yes, madam, I believe Sir William had some reason to confide in my judgment ; one little reason, perhaps.

Miss Rich. Pray, sir, what was it ?

Lof. Why, madam—but let it go no farther—it was I procured him his place.

Sir Wil. Did you, sir ?

Lof. Either you or I, sir.

Miss Rich. This, Mr. Lofty, was very kind indeed.

Lof. I did love him, to be sure ; he had some amusing qualities ; no man was fitter to be a toast-master to a club, or had a better head.

Miss Rich. A better head ?

Lof. Ay, at a bottle. To be sure, he was as dull as a choice spirit; but, hang it, he was grateful, very grateful; and gratitude hides a multitude of faults.

Sir Wil. He might have reason, perhaps. His place is pretty considerable, I'm told.

Lof. A trifle, a mere trifle among us men of business. The truth is, he wanted dignity to fill up a greater.

Sir Wil. Dignity of person, do you mean, sir? I'm told he's much about my size and figure, sir.

Lof. Ay, tall enough for a marching regiment; but then he wanted a something — a consequence of form—a kind of a—I believe the lady perceives my meaning.

Miss Rich. Oh, perfectly; you courtiers can do anything, I see.

Lof. My dear madam, all this is but a mere exchange; we do greater things for one another every day. Why, as thus, now: let me suppose you the First Lord of the Treasury; you have an employment in you that I want; I have a place in me that you want: do me here, do you there: interest of both sides, few words, flat, done and done, and it's over.

Sir Wil. A thought strikes me (*aside*). Now you mention Sir William Honeywood, madam; and as he seems, sir, an acquaintance of yours, you'll be glad to hear he's arrived from Italy. I had it from a friend who knows him as well as he does me, and you may depend on my information.

Lof. The devil he is! If I had known that, we should not have been quite so well acquainted. (*Aside.*)

Sir Wil. He is certainly returned; and, as this gentleman is a friend of yours, he can be of signal service to us, by introducing me to him: there are some papers relative to your affairs, that require dispatch and his inspection.

Miss Rich. This gentleman, Mr. Lofty, is a person employed in my affairs: I know you'll serve us.

Lof. My dear madam, I live but to serve you. Sir William shall even wait upon him, if you think proper to command it.

Sir Wil. That will be quite unnecessary.

Lof. Well, we must introduce you, then. Call upon me—let me see—ay, in two days.

Sir Wil. Now, or the opportunity will be lost for ever.

Lof. Well, if it must be now, now let it be. But damn it, that's unfortunate; my Lord Grig's cursed Pensacola business comes on this very hour, and I'm engaged to attend—another time——

Sir Wil. A short letter to Sir William will do.

Lof. You shall have it; yet, in my opinion, a letter is a very bad way of going to work; face to face, that's my way.

Sir Wil. The letter, sir, will do quite as well.

Lof. Zounds! Sir, do you pretend to direct me in the business of office? Do you know me, sir? Who am I?

Miss Rich. Dear Mr. Lofty, this request is not so much his as mine; if my commands—but you despise my power.

Lof. Delicate creature! your commands could even control a debate at midnight: to a power so constitutional, I am all obedience and tranquillity. He shall have a letter: where is my secretary? Dubardieu! And yet, I protest I don't like this way of doing business. I think if I spoke first to Sir William—but you will have it so. [*Exit with* MISS RICHLAND.

Sir Wil. (*Alone.*) Ha! ha! ha!—This, too, is one of my nephew's hopeful associates. O vanity, thou constant deceiver, how do all thy efforts to exalt, serve but to sink us! Thy false colourings, like those employed to heighten beauty, only seem to mend that bloom which they contribute to destroy. I'm not displeased at this interview: exposing this fellow's impudence to the contempt it deserves, may be of use to my design; at least, if he can reflect, it will be of use to himself.

Enter JARVIS.

Sir Wil. How now, Jarvis, where's your master, my nephew?

Jar. At his wit's ends, I believe: he's scarce gotten

out of one scrape, but he's running his head into another.

Sir Wil. How so ?

Jar. The house has but just been cleared of the bailiffs, and now he's again engaging, tooth and nail, in assisting old Croaker's son to patch up a clandestine match with the young lady that passes in the house for his sister.

Sir Wil. Ever busy to serve others.

Jar. Ay, anybody but himself. The young couple, it seems, are just setting out for Scotland ; and he supplies them with money for the journey.

Sir Wil. Money ! how is he able to supply others, who has scarce any for himself ?

Jar. Why, there it is : he has no money, that's true ; but then, as he never said *No* to any request in his life, he has given them a bill, drawn by a friend of his upon a merchant in the city, which I am to get changed ; for you must know that I am to go with them to Scotland myself.

Sir Wil. How ?

Jar. It seems the young gentleman is obliged to take a different road from his mistress, as he is to call upon an uncle of his that lives out of the way, in order to prepare a place for their reception, when they return ; so they have borrowed me from my master, as the properest person to attend the young lady down.

Sir Wil. To the land of matrimony ! A pleasant journey, Jarvis.

Jar. Ay, but I'm only to have all the fatigues on't.

Sir Wil. Well, it may be shorter, and less fatiguing, than you imagine. I know but too much of the young lady's family and connections, whom I have seen abroad. I have also discovered that Miss Richland is not indifferent to my thoughtless nephew ; and will endeavour, though I fear in vain, to establish that connection. But, come, the letter I wait for must be almost finished ; I'll let you further into my intentions, in the next room.

[*Exeunt.*

ACT THE FOURTH

Scene—Croaker's *House*.

Lof. Well, sure the devil's in me of late, for running my head into such defiles, as nothing but a genius like my own could draw me from. I was formerly contented to husband out my places and pensions with some degree of frugality ; but, curse it, of late I have given away the whole Court Register in less time than they could print the title-page : yet, hang it, why scruple a lie or two to come at a fine girl, when I every day tell a thousand for nothing. Ha ! Honeywood here before me ! Could Miss Richland have set him at liberty ?

Enter HONEYWOOD.

Mr. Honeywood, I'm glad to see you abroad again. I find my concurrence was not necessary in your unfortunate affairs. I had put things in a train to do your business ; but it is not for me to say what I intended doing.

Hon. It was unfortunate indeed, sir. But what adds to my uneasiness is, that while you seem to be acquainted with my misfortune, I myself continue still a stranger to my benefactor.

Lof. How ! not know the friend that served you ?

Hon. Can't guess at the person.

Lof. Inquire.

Hon. I have ; but all I can learn is, that he chooses to remain concealed, and that all inquiry must be fruitless.

Lof. Must be fruitless !

Hon. Absolutely fruitless.

Lof. Sure of that ?

Hon. Very sure.

Lof. Then I'll be damned if you shall ever know it from me.

Hon. How, sir !

Lof. I suppose now, Mr. Honeywood, you think my rent-roll very considerable, and that I have vast sums of money to throw away ; I know you do. The world, to be sure, says such things of me.

Hon. The world, by what I learn, is no stranger to your generosity. But where does this tend ?

Lof. To nothing ; nothing in the world. The town, to be sure, when it makes such a thing as me the subject of conversation, has asserted, that I never yet patronized a man of merit.

Hon. I have heard instances to the contrary, even from yourself.

Lof. Yes, Honeywood ; and there are instances to the contrary, that you shall never hear from myself.

Hon. Ha ! dear sir, permit me to ask you but one question.

Lof. Sir, ask me no questions ; I say, sir, ask me no questions ; I'll be damned if I answer them.

Hon. I will ask no further. My friend ! my bene-factor ! it is, it must be here, that I am indebted for freedom, for honour. Yes, thou worthiest of men, from the beginning I suspected it, but was afraid to return thanks ; which, if undeserved, might seem reproaches.

Lof. I protest I do not understand all this, Mr. Honeywood : you treat me very cavalierly. I do assure you, sir—Blood ! sir, can't a man be permitted to enjoy the luxury of his own feelings, without all this parade ?

Hon. Nay, do not attempt to conceal an action that adds to your honour. Your looks, your air, your manner, all confess it.

Lof. Confess it, sir ! Torture itself, sir, shall never

bring me to confess it. Mr. Honeywood, I have admitted
you upon terms of friendship. Don't let us fall out ;
make me happy, and let this be buried in oblivion. You
know I hate ostentation ; you know I do. Come, come,
Honeywood, you know I always loved to be a friend, and
not a patron. I beg this may make no kind of distance
between us. Come, come, you and I must be more
familiar—indeed we must.

Hon. Heavens ! Can I ever repay such friendship ?
Is there any way ?—Thou best of men, can I ever return
the obligation ?

Lof. A bagatelle, a mere bagatelle ! But I see your
heart is labouring to be grateful. You shall be grateful.
It would be cruel to disappoint you.

Hon. How ! teach me the manner. Is there any
way ?

Lof. From this moment you're mine. Yes, my friend,
you shall know it—I'm in love.

Hon. And can I assist you ?

Lof. Nobody so well.

Hon. In what manner ? I'm all impatience.

Lof. You shall make love for me.

Hon. And to whom shall I speak in your favour ?

Lof. To a lady with whom you have great interest,
I assure you : Miss Richland.

Hon. Miss Richland !

Lof. Yes, Miss Richland. She has struck the blow
up to the hilt in my bosom, by Jupiter !

Hon. Heavens ! was ever anything more unfortunate !
It is too much to be endured.

Lof. Unfortunate, indeed ! And yet I can endure it,
till you have opened the affair to her for me. Between
ourselves, I think she likes me. I'm not apt to boast,
but I think she does.

Hon. Indeed ! But, do you know the person you
apply to ?

Lof. Yes, I know you are her friend and mine : that's
enough. To you, therefore, I commit the success of

my passion. I'll say no more ; let friendship do the rest. I have only to add, that if at any time my little interest can be of service—but, hang it, I'll make no promises—you know my interest is yours at any time. No apologies, my friend, I'll not be answered ; it shall be so.   [*Exit.*

Hon. Open, generous, unsuspecting man ! He little thinks that I love her too ; and with such an ardent passion !—But then it was ever but a vain and hopeless one ; my torment, my persecution ! What shall I do ? Love, friendship ; a hopeless passion, a deserving friend ! Love, that has been my tormentor ; a friend, that has, perhaps, distressed himself to serve me. It shall be so. Yes, I will discard the fondling hope from my bosom, and exert all my influence in his favour. And yet to see her in the possession of another !—Insupportable ! But then to betray a generous, trusting friend !—Worse, worse ! Yes, I'm resolved. Let me but be the instrument of their happiness, and then quit a country, where I must for ever despair of finding my own.   [*Exit.*

Enter OLIVIA *and* GARNET, *who carries a Milliner's Box.*

Oliv. Dear me, I wish this journey were over. No news of Jarvis yet ? I believe the old peevish creature delays purely to vex me.

Gar. Why, to be sure, madam, I did hear him say, a little snubbing before marriage would teach you to bear it the better afterwards.

Oliv. To be gone a full hour, though he had only to get a bill changed in the city ! How provoking !

Gar. I'll lay my life, Mr. Leontine, that had twice as much to do, is setting off by this time from his inn ; and here you are left behind.

Oliv. Well, let us be prepared for his coming, however. Are you sure you have omitted nothing, Garnet ?

Gar. Not a stick, madam—all's here. Yet I wish you could take the white and silver to be married in. It's

the worst luck in the world, in anything but white. I
knew one Bett Stubbs, of our town, that was married
in red ; and, as sure as eggs is eggs, the bridegroom and
she had a miff before morning.

Oliv. No matter. I'm all impatience till we are out
of the house.

Gar. Bless me, madam, I had almost forgot the wedding ring !—The sweet little thing—I don't think it
would go on my little finger. And what if I put in a
gentleman's night-cap, in case of necessity, madam ?
But here's Jarvis.

Enter JARVIS.

Oliv. O Jarvis, are you come at last ? We have been
ready this half-hour. Now let's be going. Let us fly !

Jar. Ay, to Jericho ; for we shall have no going to
Scotland this bout, I fancy.

Oliv. How ! what's the matter ?

Jar. Money, money, is the matter, madam. We have
got no money. What the plague do you send me of
your fool's errand for ? My master's bill upon the city
is not worth a rush. Here it is ; Mrs. Garnet may pin
up her hair with it.

Oliv. Undone ! How could Honeywood serve us so !
What shall we do ? Can't we go without it ?

Jar. Go to Scotland without money ! To Scotland
without money ! Lord, how some people understand
geography ! We might as well set sail for Patagonia
upon a cork jacket.

Oliv. Such a disappointment ! What a base, insin-
cere man was your master, to serve us in this manner !
Is this his good-nature ?

Jar. Nay, don't talk ill of my master, madam.
I won't bear to hear anybody talk ill of him but
myself.

Gar. Bless us ! now I think on't, madam, you need
not be under any uneasiness : I saw Mr. Leontine receive
forty guineas from his father just before he set out, and

he can't yet have left the inn. A short letter will reach him there.

Oliv. Well remembered, Garnet; I'll write immediately. How's this! Bless me, my hand trembles so, I can't write a word. Do you write, Garnet; and, upon second thought, it will be better from you.

Gar. Truly, madam, I write and indite but poorly. I never was 'cute at my learning. But I'll do what I can to please you. Let me see. All out of my own head, I suppose!

Oliv. Whatever you please.

Gar. (*Writing.*) Muster Croaker—Twenty guineas, madam?

Oliv. Ay, twenty will do.

Gar. At the bar of the Talbot till called for. Expedition—Will be blown up—All of a flame—Quick dispatch—Cupid, the little god of love.—I conclude it, madam, with Cupid: I love to see a love-letter end like poetry.

Oliv. Well, well, what you please, anything. But how shall we send it? I can trust none of the servants of this family.

Gar. Odso, madam, Mr. Honeywood's butler is in the next room: he's a dear, sweet man; he'll do anything for me.

Jar. He! the dog, he'll certainly commit some blunder. He's drunk and sober ten times a day.

Oliv. No matter. Fly, Garnet; anybody we can trust will do. (*Exit* GARNET.) Well, Jarvis, now we can have nothing more to interrupt us; you may take up the things, and carry them on to the inn. Have you no hands, Jarvis?

Jar. Soft and fair, young lady. You, that are going to be married, think things can never be done too fast; but we, that are old, and know what we are about, must elope methodically, madam.

Oliv. Well, sure, if my indiscretions were to be done over again——

Jar. My life for it, you would do them ten times over.

Oliv. Why will you talk so ? If you knew how unhappy they make me——

Jar. Very unhappy, no doubt : I was once just as unhappy when I was going to be married myself. I'll tell you a story about that——

Oliv. A story ! when I'm all impatience to be away. Was there ever such a dilatory creature !——

Jar. Well, madam, if we must march, why, we will march, that's all. Though, odds bobs, we have still forgot one thing ; we should never travel without—a case of good razors, and a box of shaving-powder. But no matter, I believe we shall be pretty well shaved by the way. [*Going.*

Enter GARNET.

Gar. Undone, undone, madam. Ah, Mr. Jarvis, you said right enough. As sure as death, Mr. Honeywood's rogue of a drunken butler dropped the letter before he went ten yards from the door. There's old Croaker has just picked it up, and is this moment reading it to himself in the hall.

Oliv. Unfortunate ! We shall be discovered.

Gar. No, madam ; don't be uneasy ; he can neither make head nor tail of it. To be sure he looks as if he was broke loose from Bedlam about it, but he can't find what it means for all that. O lud, he is coming this way all in the horrors.

Oliv. Then let us leave the house this instant, for fear he should ask further questions. In the meantime, Garnet, do you write and send off just such another.

[*Exeunt.*

Enter CROAKER.

Cro. Death and destruction ! Are all the horrors of air, fire, and water to be levelled only at me ? Am I only to be singled out for gunpowder-plots, combustibles, and conflagration ? Here it is—an incendiary letter dropped at my door. " To Muster Croaker, these with speed." Ay, ay, plain enough the direction : all in the genuine incendiary spelling, and as cramp as the devil. " With speed." O, confound your speed. But let me read it once more. (*Reads.*) " Muster Croaker, as sone as yow see this, leve twenty gunnes at the bar of the Talboot tell caled for, or yowe and yower experetion will be al blown up." Ah, but too plain. Blood and gunpowder in every line of it. Blown up ! murderous dog ! all blown up ! Heavens ! what have I and my poor family done, to be all blown up ? (*Reads.*) " Our pockets are low, and money we must have." Ay, there's the reason ; they'll blow us up, because they have got low pockets. (*Reads.*) " It is but a short time you have to consider ; for if this takes wind, the house will quickly be all of a flame." Inhuman monsters ! blow us up, and then burn us ! The earthquake at Lisbon was but a bonfire to it. (*Reads.*) " Make quick dispatch, and so no more at present. But may Cupid, the little god of love, go with you wherever you go." The little god of love ! Cupid, the little god of love, go with me ! Go you to the devil, you and your little Cupid together. I'm so frightened, I scarce know whether I sit, stand, or go. Perhaps this moment I'm treading on lighted matches, blazing brimstone, and barrels of gunpowder. They are preparing to blow me up into the clouds. Murder ! we shall be all burnt in our beds ; we shall be all burnt in our beds !

Enter MISS RICHLAND.

Miss Rich. Lord, sir, what's the matter ?

Cro. Murder's the matter ! We shall all be blown up in our beds before morning.

Miss Rich. I hope not, sir.

Cro. What signifies what you hope, madam, when I have a certificate of it here in my hand ? Will nothing alarm my family ? Sleeping and eating, sleeping and eating, is the only work from morning till night in my house. My insensible crew could sleep, though rocked by an earthquake, and fry beef-steaks at a volcano.

Miss Rich. But, sir, you have alarmed them so often already; we have nothing but earthquakes, famines, plagues, and mad dogs, from year's end to year's end. You remember, sir, it is not above a month ago, you assured us of a conspiracy among the bakers, to poison us in our bread; and so kept the whole family a week upon potatoes.

Cro. And potatoes were too good for them. But why do I stand talking here with a girl. when I should be facing the enemy without? Here, John, Nicodemus, search the house. Look into the cellars, to see if there be any combustibles below; and above, in the apartments, that no matches be thrown in at the windows. Let all the fires be put out, and let the engine be drawn out in the yard, to play upon the house in case of necessity.   *[Exit.*

Miss Rich. (*Alone.*) What can he mean by all this? Yet, why should I inquire, when he alarms us in this manner almost every day? But Honeywood has desired an interview with me in private. What can he mean? or, rather, what means this palpitation at his approach? It is the first time he ever showed anything in his conduct that seemed particular. Sure he cannot mean to—but he's here.

Enter HONEYWOOD.

Hon. I presumed to solicit this interview, madam, before I left town, to be permitted——

Miss Rich. Indeed! Leaving town, sir?

Hon. Yes, madam; perhaps the kingdom. I have presumed, I say, to desire the favour of this interview,—in order to disclose something which our long friendship prompts. And yet my fears——

Miss Rich. His fears! What are his fears to mine!

(*Aside.*) We have indeed been long acquainted, sir ; very long. If I remember, our first meeting was at the French ambassador's.—Do you recollect how you were pleased to rally me upon my complexion there ?

Hon. Perfectly, madam : I presumed to reprove you for painting ; but your warmer blushes soon convinced the company that the colouring was all from nature.

Miss Rich. And yet you only meant it in your good-natured way, to make me pay a compliment to myself. In the same manner you danced that night with the most awkward woman in company, because you saw nobody else would take her out.

Hon. Yes ; and was rewarded the next night, by dancing with the finest woman in company, whom everybody wished to take out.

Miss Rich. Well, sir, if you thought so then, I fear your judgment has since corrected the errors of a first impression. We generally show to most advantage at first. Our sex are like poor tradesmen, that put all their best goods to be seen at the windows.

Hon. The first impression, madam, did indeed deceive me. I expected to find a woman with all the faults of conscious flattered beauty ; I expected to find her vain and insolent. But every day has since taught me that it is possible to possess sense without pride, and beauty without affectation.

Miss Rich. This, sir, is a style very unusual with Mr. Honeywood ; and I should be glad to know why he thus attempts to increase that vanity, which his own lessons have taught me to despise.

Hon. I ask pardon, madam. Yet, from our long friendship, I presumed I might have some right to offer, without offence, what you may refuse without offending.

Miss Rich. Sir ! I beg you'd reflect : though, I fear, I shall scarce have any power to refuse a request of yours, yet you may be precipitate : consider, sir.

Hon. I own my rashness ; but as I plead the cause of friendship, of one who loves—don't be alarmed, madam

—who loves you with the most ardent passion, whose whole happiness is placed in you——

Miss Rich. I fear, sir, I shall never find whom you mean, by this description of him.

Hon. Ah, madam, it but too plainly points him out ; though he should be too humble himself to urge his pretensions, or you too modest to understand them.

Miss Rich. Well ; it would be affectation any longer to pretend ignorance ; and I will own, sir, I have long been prejudiced in his favour. It was but natural to wish to make his heart mine, as he seemed himself ignorant of its value.

Hon. I see she always loved him (*aside*). I find, madam, you're already sensible of his worth, his passion. How happy is my friend, to be the favourite of one with such sense to distinguish merit, and such beauty to reward it !

Miss Rich. Your friend, sir ! What friend ?

Hon. My best friend—my friend Mr. Lofty, madam.

Miss Rich. He, sir !

Hon. Yes, he, madam. He is, indeed, what your warmest wishes might have formed him ; and to his other qualities he adds that of the most passionate regard for you.

Miss Rich. Amazement !—No more of this, I beg you, sir.

Hon. I see your confusion, madam, and know how to interpret it. And, since I so plainly read the language of your heart, shall I make my friend happy, by communicating your sentiments ?

Miss Rich. By no means.

Hon. Excuse me, I must ; I know you desire it.

Miss Rich. Mr. Honeywood, let me tell you, that you wrong my sentiments, and yourself. When I first applied to your friendship, I expected advice and assistance ; but now, sir, I see that it is in vain to expect happiness from him, who has been so bad an economist of his own ; and that I must disclaim his friendship who ceases to be a friend to himself. [*Exit.*

Hon. How is this ! she has confessed she loved him, and yet she seemed to part in displeasure. Can I have done anything to reproach myself with ? No ; I believe not : yet, after all, these things should not be done by a third person : I should have spared her confusion. My friendship carried me a little too far.

Enter CROAKER, *with the Letter in his hand, and* MRS. CROAKER.

Mrs. Cro. Ha ! ha ! ha ! And so, my dear, it's your supreme wish that I should be quite wretched upon this occasion ? Ha ! ha !

Cro. (*Mimicking.*) Ha ! ha ! ha ! And so, my dear, it's your supreme pleasure to give me no better consolation ?

Mrs. Cro. Positively, my dear ; what is this incendiary stuff and trumpery to me ? Our house may travel through the air like the house of Loretto, for aught I care, if I am to be miserable in it.

Cro. Would to Heaven it were converted into a house of correction for your benefit ! Have we not everything to alarm us ? Perhaps this very moment the tragedy is beginning.

Mrs. Cro. Then let us reserve our distress till the rising of the curtain, or give them the money they want, and have done with them.

Cro. Give them my money !—And pray, what right have they to my money ?

Mrs. Cro. And pray, what right then have you to my good humour ?

Cro. And so your good humour advises me to part with my money ? Why then, to tell your good humour a piece of my mind, I'd sooner part with my wife. Here's Mr. Honeywood ; see what he'll say to it. My dear Honeywood, look at this incendiary letter, dropped at my door. It will freeze you with terror ; and yet lovey here can read it—can read it, and laugh !

Mrs. Cro. Yes, and so will Mr. Honeywood.

Cro. If he does, I'll suffer to be hanged the next minute in the rogue's place, that's all.

Mrs. Cro. Speak, Mr. Honeywood ; is there anything more foolish than my husband's fright upon this occasion ?

Hon. It would not become me to decide, madam ; but, doubtless, the greatness of his terrors now will but invite them to renew their villainy another time.

Mrs. Cro. I told you he'd be of my opinion.

Cro. How, sir ! do you maintain that I should lie down under such an injury, and show neither by my tears, nor complaints, that I have something of the spirit of a man in me ?

Hon. Pardon me, sir. You ought to make the loudest complaints, if you desire redress. The surest way to have redress is to be earnest in the pursuit of it.

Cro. Ay, whose opinion is he of now ?

Mrs. Cro. But don't you think that laughing off our fears is the best way ?

Hon. What is the best, madam, few can say ; but I'll maintain it to be a very wise way.

Cro. But we're talking of the best. Surely the best way is to face the enemy in the field, and not wait till he plunders us in our very bed-chamber.

Hon. Why, sir, as to the best, that—that's a very wise way too.

Mrs. Cro. But can anything be more absurd than to double our distresses by our apprehensions, and put it in the power of every low fellow, that can scrawl ten words of wretched spelling, to torment us ?

Hon. Without doubt, nothing more absurd.

Cro. How ! would it not be more absurd to despise the rattle till we are bit by the snake ?

Hon. Without doubt, perfectly absurd.

Cro. Then you are of my opinion ?

Hon. Entirely.

Mrs. Cro. And you reject mine ?

Hon. Heavens forbid, madam ! No, sure, no reasoning can be more just than yours. We ought certainly to despise malice if we cannot oppose it, and not make the incendiary's pen as fatal to our repose as the highwayman's pistol.

Mrs. Cro. Oh ! then you think I'm quite right ?

Hon. Perfectly right.

Cro. A plague of plagues, we can't be both right ! I ought to be sorry, or I ought to be glad. My hat must be on my head, or my hat must be off.

Mrs. Cro. Certainly, in two opposite opinions, if one be perfectly reasonable, the other can't be perfectly right.

Hon. And why may not both be right, madam ? Mr. Croaker in earnestly seeking redress, and you in waiting the event with good humour ? Pray, let me see the letter again. I have it. This letter requires twenty guineas to be left at the bar of the Talbot Inn. If it be indeed an incendiary letter, what if you and I, sir, go there ; and, when the writer comes to be paid for his expected booty, seize him ?

Cro. My dear friend, it's the very thing ; the very thing. While I walk by the door, you shall plant yourself in ambush near the bar ; burst out upon the miscreant like a masked battery ; extort a confession at once, and so hang him up by surprise.

Hon. Yes, but I would not choose to exercise too much severity. It is my maxim, sir, that crimes generally punish themselves.

Cro. Well, but we may upbraid him a little, I suppose ? (*Ironically.*)

Hon. Ay, but not punish him too rigidly.

Cro. Well, well, leave that to my own benevolence.

Hon. Well, I do ; but remember that universal benevolence is the first law of nature.

[*Exeunt* HONEYWOOD *and* MRS. CROAKER.

Cro. Yes ; and my universal benevolence will hang the dog, if he had as many necks as a hydra.

ACT THE FIFTH

Scene—*An Inn.*

Enter OLIVIA *and* JARVIS.

Oliv. Well, we have got safe to the inn, however.
Now, if the post-chaise were ready——

Jar. The horses are just finishing their oats ; and,
as they are not going to be married, they choose to take
their own time.

Oliv. You are for ever giving wrong motives to my
impatience.

Jar. Be as impatient as you will, the horses must
take their own time ; besides, you don't consider, we
have got no answer from our fellow-traveller yet. If
we hear nothing from Mr. Leontine, we have only one
way left us.

Oliv. What way ?

Jar. The way home again.

Oliv. Not so. I have made a resolution to go, and
nothing shall induce me to break it.

Jar. Ay ; resolutions are well kept, when they jump
with inclination. However, I'll go hasten things
without. And I'll call, too, at the bar, to see if anything should be left for us there. Don't be in such a
plaguy hurry, madam, and we shall go the faster, I
promise you.   [*Exit* JARVIS.

Enter LANDLADY.

Land. What ! Solomon, why don't you move ? Pipes
and tobacco for the Lamb there—Will nobody answer ?

To the Dolphin : quick.   The Angel has been outrageous this half-hour.   Did your ladyship call, madam ?

Oliv. No, madam.

Land. I find, as you're for Scotland, madam—But that's no business of mine ; married, or not married, I ask no questions.   To be sure we had a sweet little couple set off from this two days ago for the same place. The gentleman, for a tailor, was, to be sure, as fine a spoken tailor as ever blew froth from a full pot.   And the young lady so bashful, it was near half an hour before we could get her to finish a pint of raspberry between us.

Oliv. But this gentleman and I are not going to be married, I assure you.

Land. May be not.   That's no business of mine ; for certain, Scotch marriages seldom turn out.—There was, of my own knowledge, Miss Macfag, that married her father's footman—Alack-a-day, she and her husband soon parted, and now keep separate cellars in Hedge Lane.

Oliv. A very pretty picture of what lies before me. (*Aside.*)

Enter LEONTINE.

Leon. My dear Olivia, my anxiety, till you were out of danger, was too great to be resisted.   I could not help coming to see you set out, though it exposes us to a discovery.

Oliv. May everything you do prove as fortunate. Indeed, Leontine, we have been most cruelly disappointed. Mr. Honeywood's bill upon the city has, it seems, been protested, and we have been utterly at a loss how to proceed.

Leon. How ! an offer of his own too.   Sure, he could not mean to deceive us ?

Oliv. Depend upon his sincerity ; he only mistook the desire for the power of serving us.   But let us think no more of it.   I believe the post-chaise is ready by this.

Land. Not quite yet : and, begging your ladyship's pardon, I don't think your ladyship quite ready for the post-chaise. The north road is a cold place, madam. I have a drop in the house of as pretty raspberry as ever was tipt over tongue. Just a thimble-full to keep the wind off your stomach. To be sure, the last couples we had here, they said it was a perfect nosegay. Ecod, I sent them both away as good-natured—Up went the blinds, round went the wheels, and drive away post-boy, was the word.

Enter CROAKER.

Cro. Well, while my friend Honeywood is upon the post of danger at the bar, it must be my business to have an eye about me here. I think I know an incendiary's look; for wherever the devil makes a purchase, he never fails to set his mark. Ha! who have we here? My son and daughter! What can they be doing here?

Land. I tell you, madam, it will do you good; I think I know by this time what's good for the north road. It's a raw night, madam.—Sir——

Leon. Not a drop more, good madam. I should now take it as a greater favour, if you hasten the horses, for I am afraid to be seen myself.

Land. That shall be done. Wha, Solomon! are you all dead there? Wha, Solomon, I say! [*Exit, bawling.*

Oliv. Well, I dread lest an expedition begun in fear, should end in repentance.—Every moment we stay increases our danger, and adds to my apprehensions.

Leon. There's no danger, trust me, my dear; there can be none. If Honeywood has acted with honour, and kept my father, as he promised, in employment till we are out of danger, nothing can interrupt our journey.

Oliv. I have no doubt of Mr. Honeywood's sincerity, and even his desires to serve us. My fears are from your father's suspicions. A mind so disposed to be alarmed without a cause, will be but too ready when there's a reason.

Leon. Why, let him, when we are out of his power. But believe me, Olivia, you have no great reason to dread his resentment. His repining temper, as it does no manner of injury to himself, so will it never do harm to others. He only frets to keep himself employed, and scolds for his private amusement.

Oliv. I don't know that ; but, I'm sure, on some occasions, it makes him look most shockingly.

Cro. (*Discovering himself.*) How does he look now ?— How does he look now ?

Oliv. Ah !

Leon. Undone !

Cro. How do I look now ?   Sir, I am your very humble servant. Madam, I am yours. What, you are going off, are you ? Then, first, if you please, take a word or two from me with you before you go. Tell me first where you are going ; and when you have told me that, perhaps I shall know as little as I did before.

Leon. If that be so, our answer might but increase your displeasure, without adding to your information.

Cro. I want no information from you, puppy : and you too, good madam, what answer have you got ? Eh ! (*A cry without, Stop him !*) I think I heard a noise. My friend Honeywood without—has he seized the incendiary ? Ah, no ; for now I hear no more on't.

Leon. Honeywood without ! Then, sir, it was Mr. Honeywood that directed you hither ?

Cro. No, sir, it was Mr. Honeywood conducted me hither.

Leon. Is it possible ?

Cro. Possible ! Why, he's in the house now, sir ; more anxious about me than my own son, sir.

Leon. Then, sir, he's a villain.

Cro. How, sirrah ! a villain, because he takes most care of your father ? I'll not bear it. I tell you I'll not bear it. Honeywood is a friend to the family, and I'll have him treated as such.

Leon. I shall study to repay his friendship as it deserves.

Cro. Ah, rogue, if you knew how earnestly he entered

into my griefs, and pointed out the means to detect them, you would love him as I do. (*A cry without, Stop him.*) Fire and fury! they have seized the incendiary: they have the villain, the incendiary in view. Stop him! stop an incendiary! a murderer! stop him! [*Exit.*

Oliv. Oh, my terrors! What can this tumult mean?

Leon. Some new mark, I suppose, of Mr. Honeywood's sincerity. But we shall have satisfaction: he shall give me instant satisfaction.

Oliv. It must not be, my Leontine, if you value my esteem or my happiness. Whatever be our fate, let us not add guilt to our misfortunes—Consider that our innocence will shortly be all that we have left us. You must forgive him.

Leon. Forgive him! Has he not in every instance betrayed us? Forced me to borrow money from him, which appears a mere trick to delay us; promised to keep my father engaged till we were out of danger, and here brought him to the very scene of our escape?

Oliv. Don't be precipitate. We may yet be mistaken.

Enter POSTBOY, *dragging in* JARVIS; HONEYWOOD *entering soon after.*

Post. Ay, master, we have him safe enough. Here is the incendiary dog. I'm entitled to the reward: I'll take my oath I saw him ask for the money at the bar, and then run for it.

Hon. Come, bring him along. Let us see him. Let him learn to blush for his crimes. (*Discovering his mistake.*) Death! what's here? Jarvis, Leontine, Olivia! What can all this mean?

Jar. Why, I'll tell you what it means: that I was an old fool, and that you are my master—that's all.

Hon. Confusion!

Leon. Yes, sir, I find you have kept your word with me. After such baseness, I wonder how you can venture to see the man you have injured?

Hon. My dear Leontine, by my life, my honour——

Leon. Peace, peace, for shame ; and do not continue to aggravate baseness by hypocrisy. I know you, sir, I know you.

Hon. Why, won't you hear me ? By all that's just I knew not——

Leon. Hear you, sir ! to what purpose ? I now see through all your low arts ; your ever complying with every opinion ; your never refusing any request : your friendship as common as a prostitute's favours, and as fallacious ; all these, sir, have long been contemptible to the world, and are now perfectly so to me.

Hon. Ha ! contemptible to the world ! that reaches me. (*Aside.*)

Leon. All the seeming sincerity of your professions, I now find, were only allurements to betray ; and all your seeming regret for their consequences, only calculated to cover the cowardice of your heart. Draw, villain !

Enter CROAKER, *out of breath.*

Cro. Where is the villain ? Where is the incendiary ? (*Seizing the* POSTBOY.) Hold him fast, the dog : he has the gallows in his face. Come, you dog, confess ; confess all, and hang yourself.

Post. Zounds ! master, what do you throttle me for ?

Cro. (*Beating him.*) Dog, do you resist ? do you resist ?

Post. Zounds ! master, I'm not he ; there's the man that we thought was the rogue, and turns out to be one of the company.

Cro. How !

Hon. Mr. Croaker, we have all been under a strange mistake here ; I find there is nobody guilty ; it was all an error ; entirely an error of our own.

Cro. And I say, sir, that you're in an error ; for there's guilt and double guilt, a plot, a damned jesuitical, pestilential plot, and I must have proof of it.

Hon. Do but hear me.

Cro. What, you intend to bring 'em off, I suppose ? I'll hear nothing.

Hon. Madam, you seem at least calm enough to hear reason.

Oliv. Excuse me.

Hon. Good Jarvis, let me then explain it to you.

Jar. What signifies explanations when the thing is done?

Hon. Will nobody hear me? Was there ever such a set so blinded by passion and prejudice? (*To the* POSTBOY.) My good friend, I believe you'll be surprised when I assure you——

Post. Sure me nothing—I'm sure of nothing but a good beating.

Cro. Come then, you, madam, if you ever hope for any favour or forgiveness, tell me sincerely all you know of this affair.

Oliv. Unhappily, sir, I'm but too much the cause of your suspicions; you see before you, sir, one that with false pretences has stepped into your family to betray it; not your daughter——

Cro. Not my daughter?

Oliv. Not your daughter—but a mean deceiver—who —support me, I cannot——

Hon. Help, she's going; give her air.

Cro. Ay, ay, take the young woman to the air; I would not hurt a hair of her head, whose ever daughter she may be—not so bad as that neither.

[*Exeunt all but* CROAKER.

Cro. Yes, yes, all's out; I now see the whole affair; my son is either married, or going to be so, to this lady, whom he imposed upon me as his sister. Ay, certainly so; and yet I don't find it afflicts me so much as one might think. There's the advantage of fretting away our misfortunes beforehand: we never feel them when they come.

Enter MISS RICHLAND *and* SIR WILLIAM.

Sir Wil. But how do you know, madam, that my nephew intends setting off from this place?

Miss Rich. My maid assured me he was come to this inn ; and my own knowledge of his intending to leave the kingdom suggested the rest. But what do I see ! my guardian here before us ! Who, my dear sir, could have expected meeting you here ? to what accident do we owe this pleasure ?

Cro. To a fool, I believe.

Miss Rich. But to what purpose did you come ?

Cro. To play the fool.

Miss Rich. But with whom ?

Cro. With greater fools than myself.

Miss Rich. Explain.

Cro. Why, Mr. Honeywood brought me here, to do nothing now I am here ; and my son is going to be married to I don't know who, that is here : so now you are as wise as I am.

Miss Rich. Married ! to whom, sir ?

Cro. To Olivia, my daughter, as I took her to be ; but who the devil she is, or whose daughter she is, I know no more than the man in the moon.

Sir Wil. Then, sir, I can inform you ; and, though a stranger, yet you shall find me a friend to your family. It will be enough at present to assure you, that both in point of birth and fortune, the young lady is at least your son's equal. Being left by her father, Sir James Wood-ville——

Cro. Sir James Woodville ! What, of the west ?

Sir Wil. Being left by him, I say, to the care of a mercenary wretch, whose only aim was to secure her fortune to himself, she was sent to France, under pretence of education ; and there every art was tried to fix her for life in a convent, contrary to her inclinations. Of this I was informed upon my arrival at Paris ; and, as I had been once her father's friend, I did all in my power to frustrate her guardian's base intentions. I had even meditated to rescue her from his authority, when your son stepped in with more pleasing violence, gave her liberty, and you a daughter.

Cro. But I intend to have a daughter of my own choosing, sir. A young lady, sir, whose fortune, by my interest with those who have interest, will be double what my son has a right to expect. Do you know, Mr. Lofty, sir?

Sir Wil. Yes, sir; and know that you are deceived in him. But step this way, and I'll convince you.

[CROAKER *and* SIR WILLIAM *seem to confer.*

Enter HONEYWOOD.

Hon. Obstinate man, still to persist in his outrage! Insulted by him, despised by all, I now begin to grow contemptible even to myself. How have I sunk by too great an assiduity to please! How have I over-taxed all my abilities, lest the approbation of a single fool should escape me! But all is now over; I have survived my reputation, my fortune, my friendships, and nothing remains henceforward for me but solitude and repentance.

Miss Rich. Is it true, Mr. Honeywood, that you are setting off, without taking leave of your friends? The report is, that you are quitting England. Can it be?

Hon. Yes, madam; and though I am so unhappy as to have fallen under your displeasure, yet, thank Heaven, I leave you to happiness; to one who loves you, and deserves your love: to one who has power to procure you affluence, and generosity to improve your enjoyment of it.

Miss Rich. And are you sure, sir, that the gentleman you mean is what you describe him?

Hon. I have the best assurances of it—his serving me. He does indeed deserve the highest happiness, and that is in your power to confer. As for me, weak and waver-ing as I have been, obliged by all, and incapable of serving any, what happiness can I find but in solitude? What hope, but in being forgotten?

Miss Rich. A thousand! to live among friends that

esteem you, whose happiness it will be to be permitted to oblige you.

Hon. No, madam, my resolution is fixed. Inferiority among strangers is easy; but among those that once were equals, insupportable. Nay, to show you how far my resolution can go, I can now speak with calmness of my former follies, my vanity, my dissipation, my weakness. I will even confess, that, among the number of my other presumptions, I had the insolence to think of loving you. Yes, madam, while I was pleading the passion of another, my heart was tortured with its own. But it is over; it was unworthy our friendship, and let it be forgotten.

Miss Rich. You amaze me!

Hon. But you'll forgive it, I know you will; since the confession should not have come from me even now, but to convince you of the sincerity of my intention of —never mentioning it more. [*Going.*

Miss Rich. Stay, sir, one moment—Ha! he here——

Enter LOFTY.

Lof. Is the coast clear? None but friends. I have followed you here with a trifling piece of intelligence; but it goes no farther; things are not yet ripe for a discovery. I have spirits working at a certain board; your affair at the Treasury will be done in less than—a thousand years. Mum!

Miss Rich. Sooner, sir, I should hope.

Lof. Why, yes, I believe it may, if it falls into proper hands, that know where to push and where to parry; that know how the land lies—eh, Honeywood!

Miss Rich. It has fallen into yours.

Lof. Well, to keep you no longer in suspense, your thing is done. It is done, I say—that's all. I have just had assurances from Lord Neverout, that the claim has been examined, and found admissible. *Quietus* is the word, madam.

Hon. But how? his lordship has been at Newmarket these ten days.

Lof. Indeed! Then Sir Gilbert Goose must have been most damnably mistaken. I had it of him.

Miss Rich. He! why Sir Gilbert and his family have been in the country this month.

Lof. This month! it must certainly be so—Sir Gilbert's letter did come to me from Newmarket, so that he must have met his lordship there; and so it came about. I have his letter about me; I'll read it to you. (*Taking out a large bundle.*) That's from Paoli of Corsica; that from the Marquis of Squilachi.—Have you a mind to see a letter from Count Poniatowski, now King of Poland?—Honest Pon—(*Searching.*) Oh, sir, what, are you here, too? I'll tell you what, honest friend, if you have not absolutely delivered my letter to Sir William Honeywood, you may return it. The thing will do without him.

Sir Wil. Sir, I have delivered it; and must inform you, it was received with the most mortifying contempt.

Cro. Contempt! Mr. Lofty, what can that mean?

Lof. Let him go on, let him go on, I say. You'll find it come to something presently.

Sir Wil. Yes, sir; I believe you'll be amazed, if after waiting some time in the ante-chamber, after being surveyed with insolent curiosity by the passing servants, I was at last assured, that Sir William Honeywood knew no such person, and I must certainly have been imposed upon.

Lof. Good! let me die; very good. Ha! ha! ha!

Cro. Now, for my life I can't find out half the goodness of it.

Lof. You can't. Ha! ha!

Cro. No, for the soul of me! I think it was as confounded a bad answer as ever was sent from one private gentleman to another.

Lof. And so you can't find out the force of the message? Why, I was in the house at that very time.

Ha! ha! It was I that sent that very answer to my own letter. Ha! ha!

Cro. Indeed! How? why?

Lof. In one word, things between Sir William and me must be behind the curtain. A party has many eyes. He sides with Lord Buzzard, I side with Sir Gilbert Goose. So that unriddles the mystery.

Cro. And so it does, indeed; and all my suspicions are over.

Lof. Your suspicions! What, then, you have been suspecting, you have been suspecting, have you? Mr. Croaker, you and I were friends; we are friends no longer. Never talk to me. It's over; I say, it's over.

Cro. As I hope for your favour I did not mean to offend. It escaped me. Don't be discomposed.

Lof. Zounds! sir, but I am discomposed, and will be discomposed. To be treated thus! Who am I? Was it for this I have been dreaded both by ins and outs? Have I been libelled in the *Gazetteer*, and praised in the *St. James's*? Have I been chaired at Wildman's, and a speaker at Merchant Tailors' Hall? Have I had my hand to addresses, and my head in the print-shops; and talk to me of suspects?

Cro. My dear sir, be pacified. What can you have but asking pardon?

Lof. Sir, I will not be pacified—Suspects! Who am I? To be used thus! Have I paid court to men in favour to serve my friends; the Lords of the Treasury, Sir William Honeywood, and the rest of the gang, and talk to me of suspects? Who am I, I say; who am I?

Sir Wil. Since, sir, you are so pressing for an answer, I'll tell you who you are. A gentleman, as well acquainted with politics as with men in power; as well acquainted with persons of fashion as with modesty; with Lords of the Treasury as with truth; and with all, as you are with Sir William Honeywood. I am Sir William Honeywood.

[Discovering his ensigns of the Bath.

Cro. Sir William Honeywood!

Hon. Astonishment! my uncle! (*Aside.*)

Lof. So then, my confounded genius has been all this time only leading me up to the garret, in order to fling me out of the window.

Cro. What, Mr. Importance, and are these your works? Suspect you! You, who have been dreaded by the ins and outs; you, who have had your hand to addresses, and your head stuck up in print-shops. If you were served right, you should have your head stuck up in a pillory.

Lof. Ay, stick it where you will; for, by the Lord, it cuts but a very poor figure where it sticks at present.

Sir Wil. Well, Mr. Croaker, I hope you now see how incapable this gentleman is of serving you, and how little Miss Richland has to expect from his influence.

Cro. Ay, sir, too well I see it; and I can't but say I have had some boding of it these ten days. So, I'm resolved, since my son has placed his affections on a lady of moderate fortune, to be satisfied with his choice, and not run the hazard of another Mr. Lofty in helping him to a better.

Sir. Wil. I approve your resolution; and here they come to receive a confirmation of your pardon and consent.

Enter MRS. CROAKER, JARVIS, LEONTINE, *and* OLIVIA.

Mrs. Cro. Where's my husband? Come, come, lovey, you must forgive them. Jarvis here has been to tell me the whole affair; and I say, you must forgive them. Our own was a stolen match, you know, my dear; and we never had any reason to repent of it.

Cro. I wish we could both say so. However, this gentleman, Sir William Honeywood, has been beforehand with you in obtaining their pardon. So, if the two poor fools have a mind to marry, I think we can tack them together without crossing the Tweed for it. (*Joining their hands.*)

Leon. How blest and unexpected! What, what can we say to such goodness? But our future obedience shall be the best reply. And as for this gentleman, to whom we owe——

Sir Wil. Excuse me, sir, if I interrupt your thanks, as I have here an interest that calls me. (*Turning to* HONEYWOOD.) Yes, sir, you are surprised to see me: and I own that a desire of correcting your follies led me hither. I saw with indignation the errors of a mind that only sought applause from others; that easiness of disposition, which, though inclined to the right, had not courage to condemn the wrong. I saw with regret those splendid errors, that still took name from some neighbouring duty; your charity, that was but injustice; your benevolence, that was but weakness; and your friendship, but credulity. I saw with regret great talents and extensive learning only employed to add sprightliness to error, and increase your perplexities. I saw your mind with a thousand natural charms; but the greatness of its beauty served only to heighten my pity for its prostitution.

Hon. Cease to upbraid me, sir: I have for some time but too strongly felt the justice of your reproaches. But there is one way still left me. Yes, sir, I have determined this very hour to quit for ever a place where I have made myself the voluntary slave of all, and to seek among strangers that fortitude which may give strength to the mind, and marshal all its dissipated virtues. Yet ere I depart, permit me to solicit favour for this gentleman; who, notwithstanding what has happened, has laid me under the most signal obligations. Mr. Lofty——

Lof. Mr. Honeywood, I'm resolved upon a reformation as well as you. I now begin to find that the man who first invented the art of speaking truth, was a much cunninger fellow than I thought him. And to prove that I design to speak truth for the future, I must now assure you, that you owe your late enlargement to another ; as, upon my soul, I had no hand in the matter. So now, if any of the company has a mind for preferment, he may take my place, I'm determined to resign.

[*Exit.*

Hon. How have I been deceived !

Sir Wil. No, sir, you have been obliged to a kinder, fairer friend, for that favour— to Miss Richland. Would she complete our joy, and make the man she has honoured by her friendship happy in her love, I shall then forget all, and be as blest as the welfare of my dearest kinsman can make me.

Miss Rich. After what is passed it would be but affectation to pretend to indifference. Yes, I will own an attachment, which I find was more than friendship. And if my entreaties cannot alter his resolution to quit the country, I will even try if my hand has not power to detain him. (*Giving her hand.*)

Hon. Heavens ! how can I have deserved all this ? How express my happiness, my gratitude ? A moment like this overpays an age of apprehensions.

Cro. Well, now I see content in every face ; but Heaven send we be all better this day three months !

Sir Wil. Henceforth, nephew, learn to respect yourself. He who seeks only for applause from without, has all his happiness in another's keeping.

Hon. Yes, sir, I now too plainly perceive my errors ; my vanity, in attempting to please all by fearing to offend any ; my meanness, in approving folly lest fools should disapprove. Henceforth, therefore, it shall be my study to reserve my pity for real distress ; my friendship for true merit ; and my love for her, who first taught me what it is to be happy.

EPILOGUE

As puffing quacks some caitiff wretch procure
To swear the pill, or drop, has wrought a cure ;
Thus, on the stage, our playwrights still depend
For Epilogues and Prologues on some friend,
Who knows each art of coaxing up the town,
And make full many a bitter pill go down.
Conscious of this, our bard has gone about,
And teased each rhyming friend to help him out.
An Epilogue, things can't go on without it ;
It could not fail, would you but set about it.
Young man, cries one (a bard laid up in clover),
Alas ! young man, my writing days are over ;
Let boys play tricks, and kick the straw, not I ;
Your brother doctor there, perhaps, may try.
What I ! dear sir, the doctor interposes ;
What, plant my thistle, sir, among his roses !
No, no, I've other contests to maintain ;
To-night I head our troops at Warwick Lane.
Go ask your manager—Who, me ! Your pardon ;
Those things are not our forte at Covent Garden.
Our author's friends, thus placed at happy distance,
Give him good words indeed, but no assistance.
As some unhappy wight at some new play,
At the pit door stands elbowing away ;
While oft, with many a smile, and many a shrug,
He eyes the centre, where his friends sit snug

His simpering friends, with pleasure in their eyes,
Sink as he sinks, and as he rises rise :
He nods, they nod ; he cringes, they grimace ;
But not a soul will budge to give him place.
Since then, unhelped, our bard must now conform
" To 'bide the pelting of this pitiless storm,"
Blame where you must, be candid where you can,
And be each critic the *Good-natured Man.*

THE END

160

PRINTED IN GREAT BRITAIN AT
THE PRESS OF THE PUBLISHERS